Effectiveness of Post-fire Burned Area Emergency Response (BAER) Road Treatments: Results from Three Wildfires

Randy B. Foltz and Peter R. Robichaud

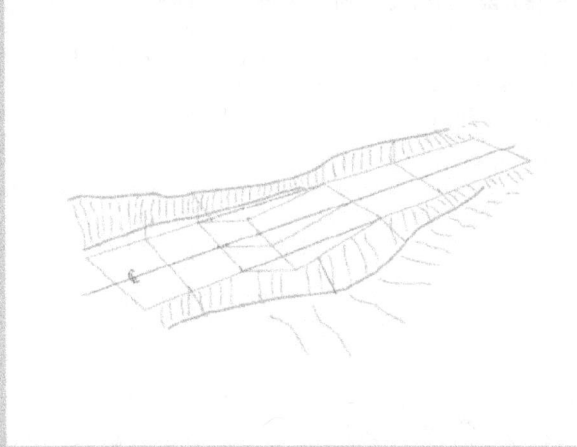

USDA United States Department of Agriculture / Forest Service

Rocky Mountain Research Station

General Technical Report RMRS-GTR-313

October 2013

Foltz, Randy B.; Robichaud, Peter, R. 2013. **Effectiveness of post-fire Burned Area Emergency Response (BAER) road treatments: Results from three wildfires**. RMRS-GTR-313. Fort Collins, CO: U.S. Department of Agriculture, Forest Service, Rocky Mountain Research Station. 40 p.

Abstract

Wildland fires often cause extreme changes in the landscape that drastically influence surface runoff and soil erosion, which can impact forest resources, aquatic habitats, water supplies, public safety, and forest access infrastructure such as forest roads. Little information is available on the effectiveness of various post-fire road treatments, thus this study was designed to evaluate common treatments implemented after fire. The 2006 Tripod Complex, 2007 Cascade Complex, and the 2008 Klamath Theater Complex Fires were selected because of their large size and extensive use of road treatments. Two of the three locations had below average precipitation and all three had precipitation that did not achieve the post-fire road treatment design storms. With this amount of precipitation testing, all of the treatments we monitored met the design objectives. All three of the locations had large soil loss in the first year after the fire followed by a quick recovery of ground cover to 40 to 50 percent at the end of year one. Soil loss from roadside hydromulch was not statistically significant from control (no treatment) on the Tripod Complex sites. Soil loss at the Cascade Complex sites was a statistically significant difference on the straw mulch compared to the control (no treatment), but there were no different pairwise differences among straw mulch, Polyacrylamide (PAM), and Woodstraw™. This suggests that the amount of cover is more important than the type of cover. Three studies and 5 years after beginning the studies, we think the best approach to assessing the effectiveness of post-fire BAER road treatments is to gain a limited knowledge of many sites along a road system rather than a detailed knowledge of a few sites.

Keywords: erosion, assessment, values at risk, recovery, road failures

Authors

Randy B. Foltz is a Research Engineer with the Air, Watershed, and Aquatic Science Program at the Rocky Mountain Research Station's Forestry Sciences Laboratory in Moscow, Idaho. His research focuses on the effects of recreation, ATVs, and other human activities on soils and water quality.

Peter R. Robichaud is a Research Engineer with the Air, Watershed, and Aquatic Science Program at the Rocky Mountain Research Station's Forestry Sciences Laboratory in Moscow, Idaho. He develops and implements research protocols for measuring and predicting post-fire runoff and erosion and post-fire treatment effectiveness.

You may order additional copies of this publication by sending your mailing information in label form through one of the following media. Please specify the publication title and number.

Publishing Services

Telephone	(970) 498-1392
FAX	(970) 498-1122
E-mail	rschneider@fs.fed.us
Web site	http://www.fs.fed.us/rmrs
Mailing Address	Publications Distribution Rocky Mountain Research Station 240 West Prospect Road Fort Collins, CO 80526

Acknowledgments

Funding for these studies came from Okanogan & Wenatchee, Payette, and Klamath National Forests. Robert Brown, Joseph Wagenbrenner, Natalie Copeland, and Troy Henseik, [Rocky Mountain Research Station (RMRS)], contributed the majority of the installation and monitoring efforts at the Tripod Complex Fires. Joseph Wagenbrenner (RMRS), Troy Henseik, and Thomas Crawford (Payette National Forest), did the majority of installation and monitoring at the Cascade Complex Fires. Natalie Copeland and Joseph Wagenbrenner were responsible for the initial data collection on the Klamath Theater Complex Fires with Ben Kopyscianski (RMRS) continuing the monitoring effort. Seasonal employees contributed valuable assistance at all three studies. The study would not have been possible without local forest and district assistance from David Colbert (Okanogan and Wenatchee National Forests), Thomas Crawford (Payette National Forest), and Greg Bousfield (Klamath National Forest). Finally, we wish to thank Meredith Webster, former Forest Service National Burned Area Emergency Response (BAER) Coordinator, Penny Luehring, Forest Service National BAER Coordinator, and Bruce Sims, Forest Service Region 1 BAER Coordinator, for the encouragement and assistance to undertake these studies.

Contents

Effectiveness of Post-fire Burned Area Emergency Response (BAER) Road Treatments: Results from Three Wildfires

Randy B. Foltz and Peter R. Robichaud

Introduction

Wildland fires, a natural process, are necessary to maintain healthy forest ecosystems; however, they cause extreme changes in the landscape that can drastically influence surface runoff and soil loss. Removal of fine fuels and the forest duff layer by combustion often causes increased runoff and subsequent increases in peak flow and sediment transport due to the loss of this protective organic material that absorbed runoff and rainfall. These increased flows can impact forest resources, aquatic habitats, water supplies, public safety, and infrastructure. Roads are one of the most impacted forest infrastructures. Road drainage features are designed to divert water to desired locations and prevent unwanted impacts. Post-fire flows often exceed design capacity, requiring that many structures be treated following fires. One frequent example is the replacement of adequately sized culverts for pre-fire conditions with larger ones that can accommodate the expected higher post-fire flows (Foltz and others 2009). Nationwide road structure replacement costs in the 1990s were about 20 percent of the total post-fire rehabilitation expense by the USDA Forest Service (Robichaud and others 2000).

Watersheds with forest and litter cover of greater than 75 percent and adequate rainfall sustain stream baseflow conditions for much or all of the year and have little or no soil loss. Fire consumes accumulated forest floor vegetation and litter thus reducing infiltration and exposing bare soil to raindrop splash erosion and overland flow (Shakesby and Doerr 2006). Runoff plot studies show that when severe fires leave less than 10 percent of the ground covered by vegetation and litter, surface runoff can increase by more than 70 percent and erosion can increase by three orders of magnitude (DeBano and others 1998; Robichaud 2005; Robichaud and others 2010).

In these changed post-fire conditions, road drainage features must accommodate increased flows to prevent infrastructure damage. Burned Area Emergency Response (BAER) teams estimate post-fire increases in stream flows and make judgments on the ability of existing road structures to accommodate the new flow regime (Foltz and others 2009). If deemed necessary, treatments are prescribed to address values-at-risk such as public safety, road infrastructure investment, and degradation of critical natural and cultural resources (Calkin and others 2007; Napper 2006).

Foltz and others (2009) synthesized post-fire road treatment information from 30 BAER team engineers, hydrologists, and soil scientists responsible for road rehabilitation decisions. Rolling dips, water bars, culvert upgrading, ditch cleaning, and ditch armoring were the most frequently recommended road treatments nationwide. With the single exception of culvert replacements, there were insufficient data available on road treatments to evaluate the effectiveness of post-fire BAER road treatments.

In response to this lack of information, the U.S. Forest Service, Rocky Mountain Research Station began a series of 3-year studies to determine the effectiveness of post-fire BAER road treatments. The first study was the 2006 Tripod Complex Fires in Washington. This 173,000 acre (70,000 ha) fire was the largest in state history and provided a large number of road treatments (U.S. Department of Agriculture 2006). The second study, in 2007, was at the Cascade Complex Fires in Idaho which burned 200,000 acres (81,000 ha) in highly erodible landforms containing Endangered Species Act spawning habitat for Chinook salmon (*Oncorhynchus tshawytscha*), steelhead (*Oncorhynchus mykiss*), and bull trout (*Salvenlinus confluentus*). The third study, in 2008, was at the 93,000 acre (38,000 ha) Klamath Theater Complex Fire in California. This fire provided a location with a climate dominated by winter frontal storms in steep terrain. This report will discuss each of the fires separately as self-contained sections and conclude with an overall summary.

2006 Tripod Complex Fires: Okanogan and Wenatchee National Forests, Washington

Introduction

The Tripod Complex Fires on the Okanogan & Wenatchee National Forests burned 173,000 acres (70,000 ha) in northeast Washington from 24 July to 26 August 2006. The fire burned in Douglas-fir (*Pseudotsuga menziesii*) and subalpine fir (*Abies lasiocarpa*) coniferous forest resulting in 24 percent high, 27 percent moderate, 47 percent low soil burn severity, and 2 percent unburned categories. Dominant soils were "sandy" skeletal derived from volcanic ash over glacial drift; the geology was volcanic ash over mixed granitic glacial outwash and till over mixed granitic and metamorphic lithologies with glacially scoured landforms. The transportation system affected consisted of 70 miles (110 km) of trails and 259 miles (417 km) of roads valued at over $17,000,000. The emergency treatment objectives were to establish conditions that protected human life, property and critical cultural/natural resources with protection of roads and trails an important objective. Treatments were proposed to ensure that existing road and trail drainage structures were able to handle expected increases in flow; proposed structural treatments to roads and trails were designed to reduce accelerated road erosion and stream sedimentation potential and to protect the road and trail infrastructure (USDA Forest Service 2006). The BAER team selected a design storm duration of 1 hour with a storm magnitude of 1.1 inches (28 mm). The road and trail recommendation consisted of 14 treatments at a total cost of $6,900,560.

The Rocky Mountain Research Station collaborated with the forest in a pilot study (1) to monitor how selected road treatments perform and determine if treatments met their objective by observing how treatments respond to rainfall and snowmelt runoff events for 3 years following the fire, and (2) to validate a methodology to assess the effectiveness of road treatments. The study focused on the seven most expensive treatments: surface repair, drain dips, drain dips with armor, ditch maintenance, replace or upgrade culvert, armor inlet/outlet of new/existing culverts, and hydromulch on road cuts and fills. The purposes of these treatments were "to (1) minimize the potential for elevated or concentration of surface runoff, mass erosion, and sediment delivery from Forest Service roads within the Tripod Complex Fire, and (2) insure public awareness of road-related and other hazards in the burned area and that road user safety features are in place. Upgrade road drainage structures to accommodate anticipated increased runoff conditions and construction of new drainage structures to improve facility drainage systems." (USDA Forest Service 2006).

FS Road 5009200 had 22 sites with treatments that included surface repair, drain dips, armored drain dips, ditch maintenance, culvert replacement, and armor culvert. The elevation range was 3000 to 4300 ft (910 to 1300 m). FS Road 3700 had 14 sites with treatments that included ditch maintenance, culvert replacement, armor culvert outlet, and hydromulch. The elevation range was 5200 to 5900 ft (1600 to 1800 m). A third road section was on FS Road 3900 with ditch maintenance, culvert replacement, armor culvert, and hydromulch. This section had an elevation range of 6000 to 6200 ft (1800 to 1900 m) (fig. 1).

Installation of equipment and monitoring of road treatments began 4 June 2007. Our study design was to randomly select six replicates of each treatment within a 3 to 5 mi (5 to 8 km) long section of road that was located in a high soil burn severity area. We hoped to maximize the opportunity to observe a test of the effectiveness of the BAER treatment and have sufficiently similar weather conditions to allow comparison of how well each replicate responded to the post-fire conditions. The Ramsey Peak FS road 5009200, the Middle Fork Boulder Creek area of the FS road 3700, and the Freezout Ridge area of the FS road 3900 best met our requirements (table 1).

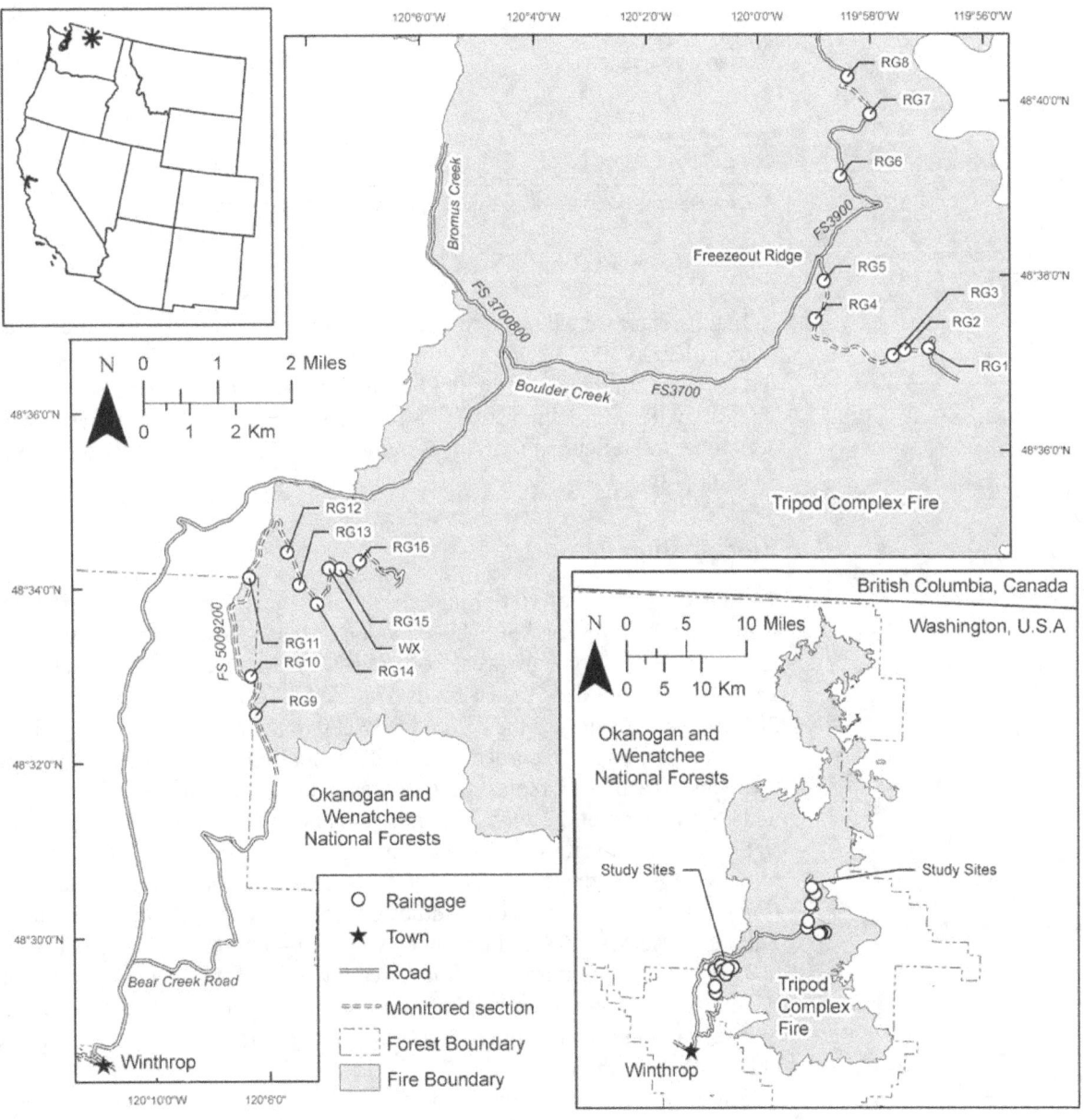

Figure 1—Map of Tripod Complex Fires showing study locations.

USDA Forest Service Gen. Tech. Rep. RMRS-GTR-313. 2013

3

Table 1—Treatment locations, replicates, and elevations.

Treatment	Replicates	FS road number	Elevation range
			(ft [m])
Surface repair	3*	5009200	3180 to 3430 [970 to 1040]
Armored dips	7	5009200	3470 to 4310 [1060 to 1310]
Culvert replacement	5	5009200, 3700, 3900	3040 to 6200 [930 to 1890]
Ditch cleaning	7	5009200, 3700, 3900	3180 to 6200 [970 to 1890]
Rolling dips	6	5009200	3460 to 4350 [1050 to 1330]
Harden drainage features	6	5009200, 3700, 3900	4120 to 6200 [1260 to 1890]
Hydromulch	8*	3700, 3900	5570 to 6000 [700 to 1830]

* - Each replicate consisted of a treatment plus an untreated control.

In this report we will refer to "Year 0" as the summer of the fire, the fall of 2006, the winter of 2006-2007, spring snowmelt, and rainfall precipitation up to 2 June 2007. We did not have equipment in the field during this period and, thus, have no observations. "Year 1" will mean 3 June 2007 to 30 September 2007. Subsequent years will run from 1 October to 30 September. This terminology reflects the number of growing seasons since the fire.

Precipitation

There was a total of 16 tipping bucket rain gauges throughout the study area. Eight were located on FS road 5009200, five on FS road 3700, and three on FS road 3900. All became operational the week of 3 June 2007. At the end of the study, 14 rain gauges were operational. All of the FS roads 3700 and 3900 rain gauges were removed 12 July 2011. The rain gauges on the FS road 5009200 remained in place through 1 March 2012. A weather station that recorded precipitation, humidity, temperature, soil moisture, wind speed and direction, and solar radiation was installed near mile post 7 on FS road 5009200 and began operation 27 June 2007 and remained in operation through 1 March 2012.

Summer precipitation for both summer periods varied from 56 to 85 percent of long-term average, i.e. dryer than average summer periods based on the summer precipitation for the three summers of the study as well as the 25-year mean precipitation at the Salmon Meadows RAWS site at an elevation of 4500 ft (1370 m) and located 11 miles (18 km) from the center of the study area (table 2). Both the precipitation amount and the number of days with precipitation appear to increase with road elevation.

The maximum 1-hour intensity observed by our rain gauge network was 0.43 in h^{-1} (11 mm h^{-1}) on the FS 3700 road in year 2. This intensity is considerably below the BAER team's design 1-hour storm of 1.1 inches (28 mm). While these conditions were favorable for the road treatments, they did not allow a reasonable test of the ability of the treatments to perform under expected high post-fire runoff conditions.

USDA Forest Service Gen. Tech. Rep. RMRS-GTR-313. 2013

Table 2—Summer precipitation at Salmon Meadows, FS road 5009200, FS road 3700, and FS road 3900 road. Values for Salmon Meadows are term (25-year) averages.

Location	Year one summer 4 Jun – 3 Oct 2007		Year two summer 1 May – 31 Oct 2008		Year three summer 1 May – 29 Sep 2009	
	Precip	Days with precip	Precip	Days with precip	Precip	Days with precip
	(in [mm])		*(in [mm])*		*(in [mm])*	
FS road 5009200	4.2 [110]	42	5.1 [130]	45	7.2 [180]	80
FS road 3700	5.3 [130]	45	8.4 [210]	66	9.0 [230]	71
FS road 3900	4.7 [120]	49	6.0 [150]	65	9.0 [230]	67
Salmon Meadows	6.6 [170]	-	6.6 [170]	-	6.6 [170]	-

Technical Paper No. 40 (Hershfield 1961) provides guidance into the return period of 1-hour and 30-minute rainfall intensities. For a 2-year, 1-hour event the rainfall intensity is 0.4 in h^{-1} (10 mm h^{-1}) increasing to 0.6 in h^{-1} (15 mm h^{-1}) for a 5-year, 1-hour event. Table 3 indicates that during the study period we observed between a 2-year and a 5-year return period rainfall duration. Similarly, TP-40 indicates that between a 5-year and a 10-year, 30-minute rainfall intensity was experienced during the study.

We observed that the 5 years prior to the fire were all below the mean precipitation at Salmon Meadows, then the year of the fire had precipitation above the mean followed by a return to below the mean precipitation for the duration of the 3-year study (table 4). Large fires like the Tripod Complex are often a result of prolonged drought conditions (Miller and others 2009). Since the fire does not change the climate, one would expect a high probability that drought conditions would continue after the fire. Precipitation at the Tripod Complex area followed this pattern.

Surface Repair Treatment

This treatment was called "Manage road surface water on maintenance level 2 road (Surface Repair)" with the treatments to include "Blade road surface, pull specific ditchline sections, remove outside berms and outslope where appropriate to improve road surface drainage. Remove rock and woody debris blocking ditchline. Some Level 2 road segments will be bladed where necessary to control water to protect the road surface, road fill or road ditch." (USDA Forest Service 2006). [Maintenance level 2 roads are open for use by high-clearance vehicles where passenger car traffic is not a consideration, and traffic volume and speeds are low. (Ruiz 2005)]. The cost for this treatment was $4,500 per mile ($2,800 per km) with 158 miles (254 km) receiving treatment.

Table 3—Maximum 1-hour, 30-minute, and 15-minute rainfall intensity values for each location. Values in **bold** denote maximum observed for a given road location.

FS road	Year	Max 1-hour		Max 30 min		Max 15-minute	
		(in h^{-1} [mm h^{-1}])	*Date*	*(in h^{-1} [mm h^{-1}])*	*Date*	*(in h^{-1} [mm h^{-1}])*	*Date*
5009200	1	0.36 [9]	19 Jul 2007	0.72 [18]	19 Jul	0.88 [22]	19 Jul
	2	**0.40 [10]**	**10 Jun 2008**	**0.74 [19]**	**1 Jul**	**1.32 [34]**	**1 Jul**
	3	0.34 [9]	3 Sep 2009	0.58 [15]	25 Jun	1.12 [28]	25 Jul
3700	1	0.31 [8]	19 Jul 2007	0.50 [13]	19 Jul	0.60 [15]	19 Jul
	2	**0.43 [11]**	**23 Jul 2008**	**0.68 [17]**	**23 Jul**	**0.84 [21]**	**23 Jul**
	3	0.36 [9]	6 Jul 2009	0.44 [11]	6 Jul	0.80 [20]	6 Jul
3900	1	**0.30 [8]**	**19 Sep 2007**	0.36 [9]	12 Sep	0.48 [12]	12 Sep
	2	**0.30 [8]**	**23 Jul 2008**	0.32 [8]	23 Jul	0.52 [13]	23 Jul
	3	0.28 [7]	30 Jul 2009	**0.42 [11]**	**30 Jul**	**0.56 [14]**	**30 Jul**

USDA Forest Service Gen. Tech. Rep. RMRS-GTR-313. 2013

5

Table 4—Annual precipitation at Salmon Meadows from years before Tripod Complex Fires to 3 years after.

Year	Precipitation	Rank in 30-yr of record	Above or below 30-yr mean of 22.3 in [566 mm]
	(in [mm])		
2001	10.0 [254]	27	Below by 12.3 [312]
2002	17.6 [447]	23	Below by 4.7 [119]
2003	18.6 [472]	21	Below by 3.7 [94]
2004	21.0 [533]	13	Below by 1.3 [33]
2005	17.5 [445]	24	Below by 4.8 [122]
2006 fire year	27.2 [691]	5	Above by 4.9 [124]
2007	19.0 [483]	18	Below by 3.3 [84]
2008	18.0 [457]	22	Below by 4.3 [109]
2009	16.8 [427]	25	Below by 5.5 [140]

The surface repair treatment included a limited number of road sections where aggregate was placed on the road in order to minimize the concentration of surface runoff by reducing the formation of wheel ruts. These aggregate placement sections on roads with planned salvage logging allowed us a unique opportunity to compare these two surface repair treatments under conditions of heavy truck traffic. In 2007 we measured FS road 5009200 cross-sections on three 50 ft (15 m) long sections with aggregate and three adjacent similar sections without aggregate. All sections had a well-defined crown and sufficient out slopes to allow runoff drainage. Two traffic counters were installed in August 2008 to relate traffic to wheel rut development.

We observed no rutting of any of the aggregate test sections nor in any of the native surface sections. Most of the change in cross-section on the aggregate surface section was from movement of the individual aggregate particles rather than deepening of the wheel track (fig. 2). Although salvage logging on FS road 5009200 did occur, most of the logging truck traffic did not cross our test sections. The predominant traffic on FS road 5009200 was from hunters in pickup trucks in October of each year. Between 2400 and 4000 vehicles passed over our test sections.

Thus, application of aggregate surfacing was successful in meeting the objective of minimizing the concentration of surface runoff by reducing the formation of wheel ruts. Additionally, the adjacent native surface road sections did not form wheel ruts either.

Armored Dips

The purpose of the armored dips was to construct drain dips with the outslopes armored with Class 3 riprap (table 5) to reduce the potential for runoff concentration and accelerated surface erosion. The cost for this treatment was $4000 per mile ($2500 km^{-1}) with 83 miles (134 km) being treated.

Our monitoring consisted of randomly selecting seven armored dips on FS road 5009200 and conducting a longitudinal survey of the road for the entire length of the armored dip as well as the adjacent cutslope for about 60 ft (18 m) in the uphill direction. We did this detailed survey so that we would have the dimensions of the armored dip in the event it failed to meet the objective. From the pre-failure and any post-failure dimensions, we would be able to infer conclusions about what portion of the dip contributed to the failure. At each subsequent site visit we visually assessed whether there had been any erosion or evidence of flow in the dip. Additionally, we measured the major axis of at least 30 of the riprap rocks to compare them to the forest's class 3 riprap specification. Characterization of the riprap rock was performed at the beginning and at the end of the study.

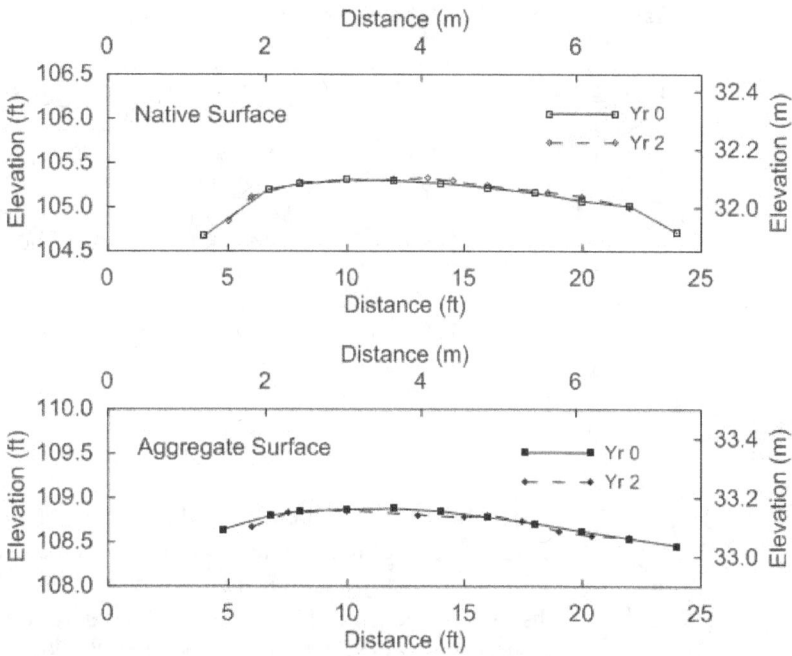

Figure 2—Cross-section of native surface and aggregate surface road at Tripod Complex Fires before (Yr 0) and after (Yr 2) 4000 vehicle passes.

Table 5—Okanogan and Wenatchee National Forest specification for Class 3 riprap rock.

Percent of rock by mass	Mass	Approximate cubic dimension[a,b]
	(pounds [kg])	(ft [m])
20	220 to 330 [100 to 150]	1.2 to 1.3 [0.36 to 0.41]
30	110 to 220 [50 to 100]	0.83 to 1.2 [0.25 to0. 36]
40	11 to 110 [5 to 50]	0.42 to 0.83 [0.13 to 0.25]
10	0 to 11[0 to 5]	0 to 0.42 [0 to 0.13]

[a] The volume of a rock with these cubic dimensions has a mass approximately equal to the specified rock mass.
[b] Furnish rock with breadth and thickness at least one-third its length.

The forest's specification for rolling dips calls for a length between 112 and 122 ft (34 and 37 m) and a depth at the fillslope edge of 0.66 ft (0.2 m). All seven of the armored dips we measured were somewhat longer, ranging from 129 to 190 ft (39 to 58 m). Six of the seven were somewhat deeper than the specification with depths ranging from 1.2 to 5.0 ft (0.4 to 1.5 m) with the remaining one only 0.3 ft (0.09 m) deep (table 6). The extra length and depth may have been in response to the anticipated additional runoff due to the post-fire conditions.

The forest's specification for class 3 riprap rock was in terms of rock mass and a length:width:thickness ratio. Converting these specifications to dimensions resulted in a length range of 1.1 to 1.5 ft (0.3 to 0.4 m). We observed that road grader maintenance cast a portion of the road material over the fill and onto the riprap armor at mile marker 7.368 essentially burying it before we could make measurements. One other armored dip, mile marker 7.353, had a fill slope too steep for us to safely walk on to take measurements. Only one of the four armored dips that we were able to measure were within the calculated length range (Table 6) with the remaining three having smaller than class 3 riprap.

Table 6—Armored dip dimensions measured at FS road 5009200 fill slope edge.

Road grade	Mile marker	Length of dip	Depth of dip	Riprap major axis	
				Initial	Final
(percent)		---------- (ft [m]) ----------			
1.1	7.329	129 [39]	1.4 [0.43]	0.74 [0.23]	0.72 [0.22]
3.8	3.842	190 [58]	1.2 [0.37]	1.25 [0.38]	1.19 [0.36]
4.6	7.431	138 [42]	2.9 [0.88]	ND	
5.6	7.353	140 [43]	2.1 [0.64]	0.63 [0.19]	ND
6.3	6.185	164 [50]	4.7 [1.4]	ND	
7.0	7.368	150 [46]	5.0 [1.5]	ND	
7.6	5.805	138 [42]	0.3 [0.09]	0.66 [0.20]	0.48 [0.15]

ND – no data

We observed no movement of the riprap rock during the study period. Further, there was no meaningful difference between initial and final riprap lengths.

There was only one evidence of flow on any of armored dips. On 24 July 2007 we observed evidence of flow from the high soil burn severity area onto the armored dip located at mile post 7.431 on FS road 5009200. The rain gauge located 330 ft (100 m) uphill recorded a 30-minute intensity of 0.56 inches h^{-1} (14 mm h^{-1}) on 18 July. The four rain gauges within a mile (0.6 km) had 30-minute intensities ranging from 0.42 to 0.68 inches h^{-1} (11 to 17 mm h^{-1}) and produced no evidence of runoff onto the road. Subsequent 30-minute intensities from the rain gauge closest to the armored dip at mile post 7.431 were 1 July 2008 of 0.56 inches h^{-1} (14 mm h^{-1}) and on 25 July 2009 one of 0.58 inches h^{-1} (15 mm h^{-1}). Neither of these later rainfall intensities produced visible runoff suggesting that the burned area had recovered sufficiently to not produce runoff or the rainfall intensities were not high enough to produce runoff.

Thus, the armored dips were successful in meeting the objective of reducing the potential for runoff concentration and accelerated surface erosion. At least 0.6 inches h^{-1}, 30 minute (15 mm h^{-1}, 30-minute) duration rainfall was required to produce runoff from a high soil burn severity area during the first year after the fire, but that runoff did not occur from similar 30-minute duration rainfall events in subsequent years.

Culvert Replacement

The removal and replacement of damaged ditch relief or drainage culverts was the stated purpose of this treatment. The cost for this treatment was $2,000 per mile ($1,200 km^{-1}) with 158 miles (254 km) being treated.

We randomly chose two culvert replacements on FS road 5009200, three on FS road 3700, and one on FS road 3900 for a total of six. The replacement sizes ranged from 16 to 84 inches diameter (41 to 213 cm) (table 7). We measured the flow from each culvert periodically during the study. On FS road 5009200 at mile markers 1.650, and 2.219, on FS road 3700 at mile marker 19.38, and on FS road 3900 at mile marker 24.758 we installed staff gauges to correlate flow depth and discharge by developing a rating curve. We conducted a longitudinal survey of the road for the entire road length spanning the stream as well as three cross-sections of the drainage upstream from the culvert.

The BAER Implementation Team performed the replacements on FS road 5009200 prior to our monitoring. According to our measurements, the three replacements on FS road 3700 were not done, which left only the FS road 3900 replacement to be done after our monitoring began.

Table 7—Culvert dimensions and flows for selected road crossings.

Road	Mile marker	Before replacement Diameter	Before replacement Capacity	After replacement Diameter	After replacement Capacity	Slope	Measured flow Peak	Measured flow Base
		(in [cm])	*(cfs [m³ s⁻¹])*	*(in [cm])*	*(cfs [m³ s⁻¹])*	*(%)*	*(in [cm])*	*(cfs [m³ s⁻¹])*
5009200	1.650	24 [61]	11 [0.31]	84 [213]	39 [1.1]	15.4	0 [0]	0 [0]
5009200	2.219	18 [46]	1.8 [0.051]	48 [122]	13 [0.36]	12.4	0 [0]	0 [0]
3700	17.79	16 [41][a]	1.6 [0.045]	16 [41][a]	1.6 [0.045]	3.4	0.014 [0.00040]	0 [0]
3700	19.83	16 [41][a]	1.6 [0.045]	16 [41][a]	1.6 [0.45]	16.9	0.14 [0.0040]	0.03 [0.0008]
3700	19.98[b]	-	-	-	-	-	-	-
3900	24.758	2 x 24 [61]	22 [0.623]	12'7" [383] span, 4'10" [147] rise	200 [5.7]	3.2	20 [0.57]	0.3 [0.008]

[a] Culvert was not replaced.
[b] We found the construction stake, but there was no culvert and none was ever installed.

The largest culvert replacement was on FS road 5009200 at mile marker 1.650 where a 24-inch diameter (61 cm) culvert was replaced with an 84-inch (213 cm) diameter culvert. The channel was wide, 15 ft (4.6 m), but did not have sufficient flow for measurement. In 2009, the last year of our monitoring, we observed a small quantity of sand in the inlet of the culvert, but there was no other indication of flow. The maximum 30-minute rainfall intensity during the first year of the study was 0.50 inches h⁻¹ (13 mm h⁻¹) followed by a 0.74 inches h⁻¹ (19 mm h⁻¹), 30-minute intensity in year two.

A 48-inch (122 cm) diameter culvert replaced an 18-inch (46 cm) diameter culvert at mile post 2.219 on FS road 5009200. We did not measure or observe any evidence of flow in this culvert either. At this location, the maximum 30-minute rainfall in the first year was 0.50 inches h⁻¹ (13 mm h⁻¹) and a 0.58 inches h⁻¹ (15 mm h⁻¹), 30-minute duration rainfall in the second year.

The culvert at mile marker 17.79 on FS road 3700 did not get replaced. It drained both a small drainage and the adjacent road ditch where the distance between ditch outlets was 800 ft (240 m). The maximum flow we observed was 0.014 cfs (0.0040 m³ s⁻¹) with a minimum of no flow.

The culvert at mile marker 19.83 on FS road 3700 did not get replaced either. It was a ditch relief culvert with 260 ft (79 m) to the next up-the-road culvert. A spring on the burned hillside kept water flowing in the ditch essentially year-round. We installed a staff gauge in the ditch near the culvert inlet, but sediment repeatedly covered the base of the gauge. The highest flow we measured was 0.14 cfs (0.0040 m³ s⁻¹).

We found the construction stake for the culvert at mile marker 19.98, but there was no existing culvert and none was ever installed. The ditch line always appeared dry.

The most significant culvert replacement we observed was at mile marker 24.758 on FS road 3900 where two 24-inch (61 cm) diameter culverts were replaced by a single 12-ft 7 inch span by 4-ft 10-inch rise (383 cm span by 147 cm rise) single pipe. At this site, the stream was large enough to allow us to take current meter measurements and install a staff gauge. We estimated the capacity of two 24 inch culverts with unobstructed inlets to be 22 cfs (0.062 m³ s⁻¹). The capacity of the two culverts at mile marker 24.758 would be less than this value because one of the culverts had an inlet obstructed by rocks

USDA Forest Service Gen. Tech. Rep. RMRS-GTR-313. 2013

9

and was not aligned with the incoming flow. We measured a flow of 14 cfs (0.40 m³ s⁻¹) on the falling limb of the snowmelt hydrograph prior to the culvert replacement. This flow was near the capacity of the two culverts, but we did not observe evidence that the road had overtopped. After the culvert replacement we measured a flow of 20 cfs (0.57 m³ s⁻¹) again on the falling limb of the snowmelt hydrograph. This flow would likely have exceeded the capacity of the original two culverts and overtopped the road. The capacity of the replacement culvert is at least 200 cfs (5.7 m³ s⁻¹), which is 10 times the highest measured flow. This culvert replacement is one of the few instances in this study where we have evidence that without the road treatments the values-at-risk (existing road) would not have been protected.

One of the six culvert upgrades was necessary to accommodate the post-fire flows and protect the road infrastructure. That instance was in a perennial stream with a base flow of 0.3 cfs (0.008 m³ s⁻¹). If we use the three culvert upgrades that did not get done as unintended examples of not performing the recommended upgrades, three of the six upgrades were not necessary. Finally, two instances where the culvert was upgraded had no flow during the study period. In these two instances, the original much smaller culvert would have accommodated the observed flows.

Road Ditch Cleaning

The purpose of ditch cleaning was to clean or reconstruct ditches in order to accommodate anticipated increased runoff conditions and construction of new drainage structures to improve existing facility drainage systems. Cost for ditch cleaning was $4500 per mile ($2,800 km⁻¹) with 158 miles (254 km) of treatment.

We monitored the ditch cleaning treatment by measuring the depth, top width, and slope every 30 ft (10 m) on seven randomly selected treatments along three roads. FS roads 5009200 and 3700 had three sections each while FS road 3900 road had one section. We also noted if there was any loose material or obstructions in the ditch that would reduce its capacity.

Forest specifications for ditches are a top width of 3 ft (1 m) and a depth of 1 ft (0.3 m). The ditch treatments we measured were typically slightly shallower and wider than the specification (table 8).

At the beginning of our study, essentially all ditches were free of blockage. Following the aerial application of straw mulch, the ditches on FS road 5009200 in the mulch zones contained large amounts of straw mulch. As the summer progressed, pine cones and soil slumps fell into many ditch sections. These obstructions could have diverted the ditch flow onto the road surface and bypassed the ditch relief culverts. Even though the ditches were slightly shallower and many had debris, we saw no evidence that the ditches we monitored failed to convey water to the outlets.

Table 8—Ditch dimensions and obstructions

Road	Mile marker	Length	Slope	Top width	Depth
		- (ft [m]) -	(percent)	- - - - - - - (ft [m]) - - - - - - -	
5009200	22.19	292 [89.0]	4.2	3.27 [1.00]	0.41 [0.12]
	23.00	517 [158	9.1	2.65 [0.81]	0.48 [0.15]
	25.42	632 [193]	6.6	2.56 [0.78]	0.54 [0.16]
3700	19.96	259 [78.9]	8.8	4.36 [1.33]	1.09 [0.33]
	20.01	65 [20.0]	8.7	3.30 [1.01]	0.55 [0.17]
	20.21	171 [52.0]	8.5	2.92 [0.80]	0.68 [0.21]
3900	24.758	355 [108]	ND	4.14 [1.26]	0.70 [0.21]

ND – no data

Thus, the ditches cleaned immediately after the fire to a depth of about 1 ft were successful in conveying road and upland runoff. Three years after the fire with the subsequent addition of pine cones and debris, the ditches were still able to convey the observed road and upland runoff.

Drain Dips

The purpose of the drain dips was to reduce the potential for increased runoff concentration and accelerated surface erosion. Drain dips are constructed in the road running surface in order to prevent water from flowing down the road (fig. 3). The cost was estimated at $4,000 per mile ($2,500 km^{-1}) with 158 miles (254 km) being treated.

Monitoring the drain dips consisted of randomly selecting six locations on FS road 5009200 road and conducting a longitudinal survey of the road plus the adjacent cutslope for about 60 ft (18 m) in the uphill direction. This detailed survey provided us with the dimensions of the drain dip in the event it failed to meet the objective. From the pre-failure and any post-failure dimensions, we would be able to infer conclusions about what portion of the dip contributed to the failure. At each subsequent site visit we visually assessed whether there had been any erosion or evidence of flow in the drain dip.

The forest's specification for drain dips is a length of between 112 and 122 ft (34 and 37 m) with a depth at the fillslope edge of 0.66 ft (0.2 m). Similar to the armored dips, all six of the drain dips were longer and deeper than the forest's specifications (table 9), which may have been in anticipation of increased runoff.

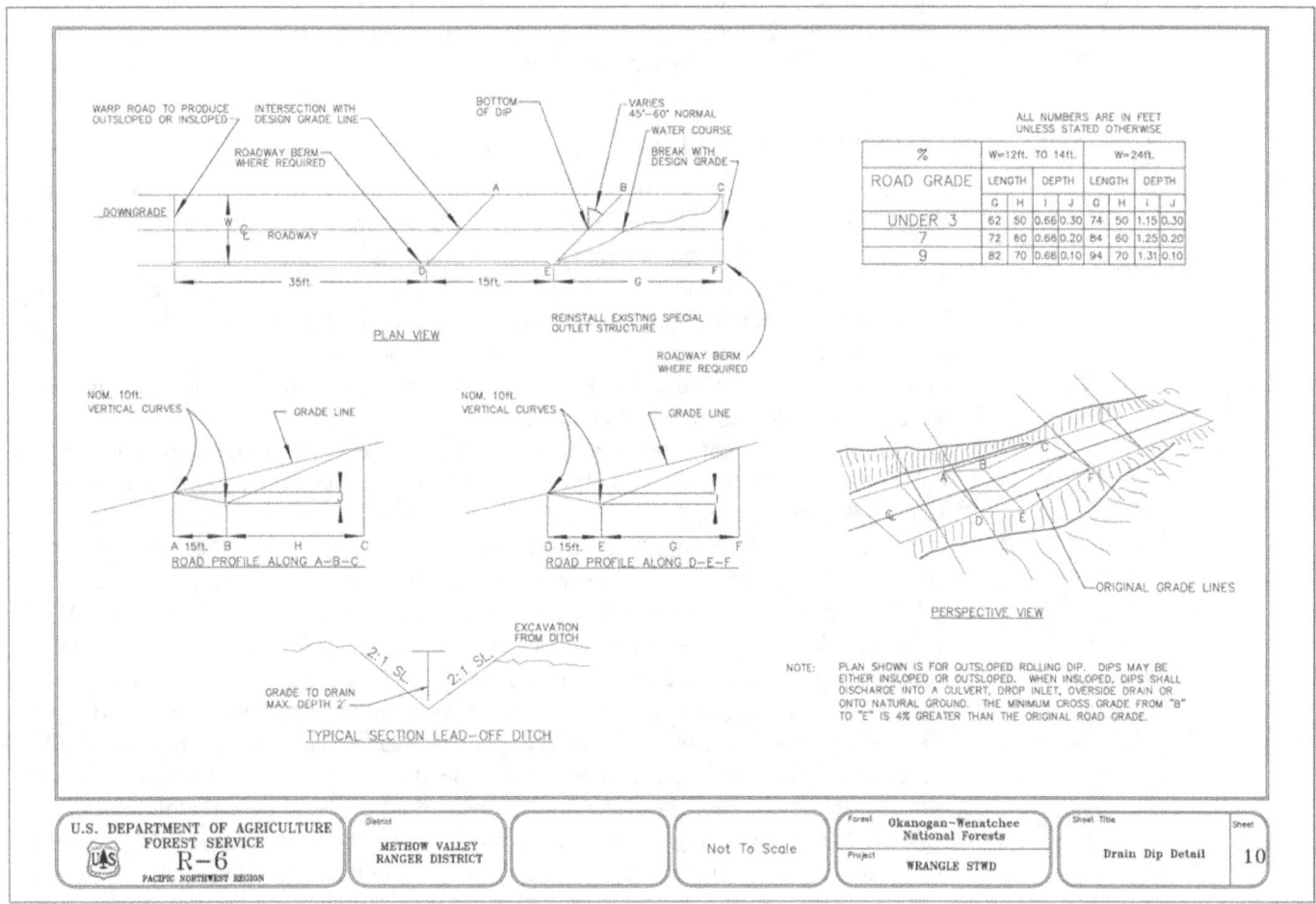

Figure 3—Drain dip specification at Tripod Complex Fires.

USDA Forest Service Gen. Tech. Rep. RMRS-GTR-313. 2013

11

Table 9—Drain dip dimensions measured at FS road 5009200 fill slope edge.

Road grade	Mile marker	Length of drain dip	Depth of drain dip	Upslope contributing Area
(percent)		------------- (ft [m]) -------------		------- (ac [ha]) -------
3.0	4.132	167 [50.9]	2.5 [0.76]	1.89 [0.77]
3.8	7.554	133 [40.6]	1.5 [0.46]	0.35 [0.14]
3.9	7.187	127 [38.6]	2.2 [0.67]	0.23 [0.092]
5.6	5.369	176 [53.6]	2.4 [0.73]	1.29 [0.52]
7.6	5.137	192 [58.6]	1.7 [0.52]	1.01 [0.41]
8.2	5.510	152 [46.3]	2.1 [0.64]	1.12 [0.45]

The maximum 30-minute rainfall intensity near any of the six drain dips during the first year was 0.68 inches h^{-1} (17 mm h^{-1}). We did not observe any evidence of runoff on the drain dips implying that a rainfall intensity of greater than 0.68 inches h^{-1} (17 mm h^{-1}) was necessary to produce runoff in a high soil burn severity forest in the first year after the fire. In years two and three, the maximum 30-minute rainfall near the six drain dips was also 0.68 inches h^{-1} (17 mm h^{-1}). No runoff onto the drain dips was observed from this storm. All six of the monitored drain dips appeared to respond to the precipitation events as intended. Because there were no storms sufficient to produce runoff, road sections without drain dips at these locations would have responded equally well.

The drain dips were successful in meeting the objective of reducing the potential for runoff concentration and accelerated surface erosion. A 30-minute rainfall intensity of 0.68 inches h^{-1} (17 mm h^{-1}) was insufficient to produce runoff from the untreated, high soil burn severity hillslopes in years 2 and 3.

Harden Drainage Features

This treatment was called both "Armor Inlet/Outlet (new/exist Corrugated Metal Pipe CMP)" and "Harden Drainage Features." The purpose was to armor with class 3 riprap to protect catch basin on inlet and to dissipate energy from the outlet." (USDA Forest Service 2006) The cost was $3,600 per mile ($2,200 km^{-1}) with 158 miles (254 km) being treated. Catch basin in this context refers to the area around the culvert inlet. In some cases the area is enlarged by removing soil to provide a settling basin for upslope runoff. When this ponded water accelerates into the culvert, it can cause erosion. The armor riprap was placed to reduce this erosion.

To monitor this treatment we randomly selected one location on FS road 5009200, four on FS road 3700, and one on FS road 3900. We measured the major axis of at least 30 of the riprap rocks on either culvert inlets or outlets to compare them to the forest's class 3 riprap specification. We noted whether or not there was any movement of the riprap rock. Additionally, we measured culvert flow periodically during the study.

Three of the six locations we chose did not receive riprap rock placement. All of these were low flow intermittent relief culverts. Of the three remaining ones, two of them had riprap rock somewhat smaller than the forest's class 3 riprap range of 1.1 to 1.5 ft (0.3 to 0.4 m) (table 10). Both of these were on culvert inlets where we did not observe any flow. The riprap rock on the Browns Meadow stream (mile marker 24.758 on FS road 3900) was larger than the class 3 specification by a small amount. This was probably beneficial because of the higher flows of 20 cfs (0.57 m^3 s^{-1}) at that location.

We did not observe any evidence of erosion in the catch basins or the culvert outlets of any of the six selected culverts. Further there was no movement of riprap and there was no difference between riprap dimension at the beginning and end of the study.

Table 10—Flow rates and riprip rock dimension for harden drainage features treatments.

FS road	Mile marker	Flow rate Maximum	Flow rate Minimum	Riprap major axis
		- - - - - - - - (cfs [m³ s⁻¹]) - - - - - - - -		- - (ft [m])- -
5009200	6.120	0 [0]	0 [0]	0.63 [0.19]
3700	17.23	0.007 [0.0002]	0 [0]	a
	17.64	0 [0]	0 [0]	0.64 [0.20]
	18.58	0.33 [0.0093]	0.041 [0.0012]	a
	18.61	0 [0]	0 [0]	a
3900	24.758	20 [0.57]	0.30 [0.0085]	1.70 [0.52]

ᵃ Installation of new riprap did not occur.

The placement of class 3 riprap rock met the objective of providing protection to culvert catch basins and outlets. If we use the three instances that did not receive riprap rock as unintended examples of not performing the hardening, we conclude that 50 percent of the recommended culvert hardenings were not necessary to handle the observed post-fire runoff. Finally, in the two instances where the culverts that did have hardening and received little or no flow during the study period, the original culvert inlet and outlets would have been sufficient as post-fire storms were insufficient to produce runoff.

Roadside Hydromulch Treatment

This treatment was called both "Hydro-seed" and "Roadside Seeding (Hydromulch)" (USDA Forest Service 2006). The seed mix was 60 percent hard fescue (Durar) *Festuca trachyphylla*, 18 percent slender wheatgrass (Adnac) *Elymus trachycaulus*, 15 percent blue wild rye *Elymus glaucus*, and 7 percent mountain brome (Bromar) *Bromus marginatus* with a total of 20.3 seeds ft⁻² (218 seeds m⁻²). We shall refer to the hydromulch and seed mix as roadside hydromulch. The objective was "to provide competition for invasive plants and to minimize erosion on roads within the Riparian Reserve" (USDA Forest Service 2006). The cost was $3,040 per mile ($1,900 km⁻¹) with 130 miles (210 km) receiving treatment.

The experimental design for the roadside hydromulch effectiveness was a randomized block. Two blocks were installed on FS road 3700 and one block on FS road 3900. Blocks on FS road 3700 contained two control and two hydromulch sections while blocks on FS road 3900 contained four control and four hydromulch sections. Each section was 25 ft (7.6 m) in length parallel to the road with a height equal to the cutslope. On FS road 3700, the cutslope heights averaged 15 ft (4.5 m) while on FS road 3900 they averaged 5 ft (1.5 m). In addition to the differences in height, the sections had different cutslope steepness values and aspects. Although the intent had been to apply the same amount of roadside hydromulch to all cutslopes, the application rate on FS road 3900 was more than twice that compared to FS road 3700. Table 11 details the differences between sections on the two roads. Our observation of cutslope characteristics and roadside hydromulch application rates on other sections of both FS roads 3700 and 3900 suggest that these differences were typical for the Tripod Complex Fires.

Table 11—Average plot characteristics for control and roadside hydromulch treatments.

FS road	Slope (percent) Cutslope	Slope (percent) Forest floor	Cutslope height	Aspect	Initial roadside hydromulch cover
			(ft [m])	*(degrees)*	*(percent)*
3700	63	46	15 [4.6]	156 & 316	29
3900	79	23	5 [1.5]	48	58

USDA Forest Service Gen. Tech. Rep. RMRS-GTR-313. 2013

13

Silt fences were installed at the base of the cutslopes to collect both dry ravel and storm generated sediment as described in Robichaud and Brown (2002). We weighed the sediment collected by the silt fences every 2 weeks for the first year and monthly thereafter. Samples were taken to correct the field measured wet weight to dry weight. We calculated the sediment mitigation effectiveness of the roadside hydromulch treatment using equation 1.

$$Mitigation = \frac{(Control - Treatment)}{Control} \qquad \text{eqn 1.}$$

where Control is the cumulative sediment from the control plots and Treatment is the cumulative sediment from the treatment plots.

We measured the ground cover on the cutslope and the burned forest floor immediately above each of the roadside hydromulch plots to assess the recovery of plant cover and the decay of the hydromulch. Three locations on the cutslopes and six locations on the forest floor were photographed at the beginning and end of each growing season. These photographs were used to determine ground cover of hydromulch, plant, litter, straw mulch, or rock using an 11- by 7.8-inch (28- by 20-cm) grid with 48 equally spaced points scaled to the photograph.

A mixed model investigated the effect of treatments (control and roadside hydromulch), the effect of time (years one through three), and the interactions among treatments and time (how treatments changed with time). The soil loss from roadside hydromulch to that of a control was analyzed using a general linear mixed model (Littell 2006). Treatments were fixed effects. Random effects were blocks, treatment by block interaction, treatment by block interaction within road, and year by treatment by block interaction. Least squares means were adjusted using the Tukey-Kramer Honest Significant Difference (HSD) to detect paired differences. A 95 percent confidence level was used for both the mixed model and the HSD adjustments. After a fourth root transformation, the mixed effects model assumed a Gaussian distribution for the soil loss.

Statistical analysis of how each plant plus litter, and mulch plus plant and litter changed over time and the impact of the hydromulch on plant regeneration were performed separately using a generalized linear mixed model with fixed and random effects in the same manner as the soil loss analysis with the exception that no transformations of the cover were required.

Initial roadside hydromulch cover averaged 44 percent and declined to 2 percent after 3 years (fig. 4a) Plant plus litter reached a maximum of nearly 50 percent at the end of the second growing season (fig. 4b). There was no statistically significant difference in plant plus litter between the control and roadside hydromulch. The combination of hydromulch cover and plant plus litter comprises the effective ground cover, a measure of protection from raindrop erosion. The roadside hydromulch mix contained grass seed, but while the measured effective ground cover was higher on the roadside hydromulch plots compared to the control plots, the only statistically significant difference was in the first year immediately after application of the roadside hydromulch (fig. 4c). The predominant ground cover on the control plots was forbs compared to grasses on the hydromulch plots (figs. 5 and 6).

The upland pre-fire forested sections did not receive intentional aerial straw mulch application. However, two of the four FS road 3700 plots received accidental aerial straw mulch application of less than 20 percent ground cover. This unintended aerial straw mulch application changed with time from an initial cover of 10 percent to less than 1 percent at the end of the study (fig. 7a). Plant plus litter and effective ground cover peaked after the end of the second growing season at 40 percent (figs. 7b and c). This peak was about 10 percentage points less than the hydromulch cutslope plots.

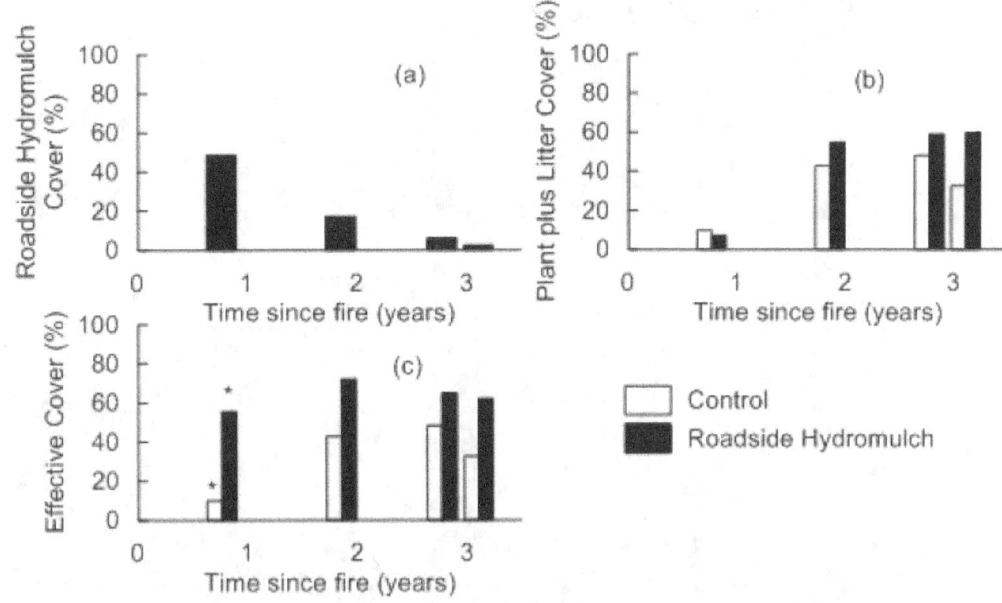

Figure 4—Cutslope cover vs. time on Tripod Complex Fires: (a) roadside hydromulch cover, (b) plant plus litter cover, and (c) effective ground cover (roadside hydromulch plus plant plus litter). Asterisks indicate statistically significant differences between control and roadside hydromulch.

Figure 5—FS road 3700, Tripod Complex Fires, cutslope with no treatment (control) test section after 3 years. Note the predominance of forbs.

USDA Forest Service Gen. Tech. Rep. RMRS-GTR-313. 2013

15

Figure 6—FS road 3700, Tripod Complex Fires, cutslope with roadside hydromulch test section after 3 years. Note the predominance of grasses.

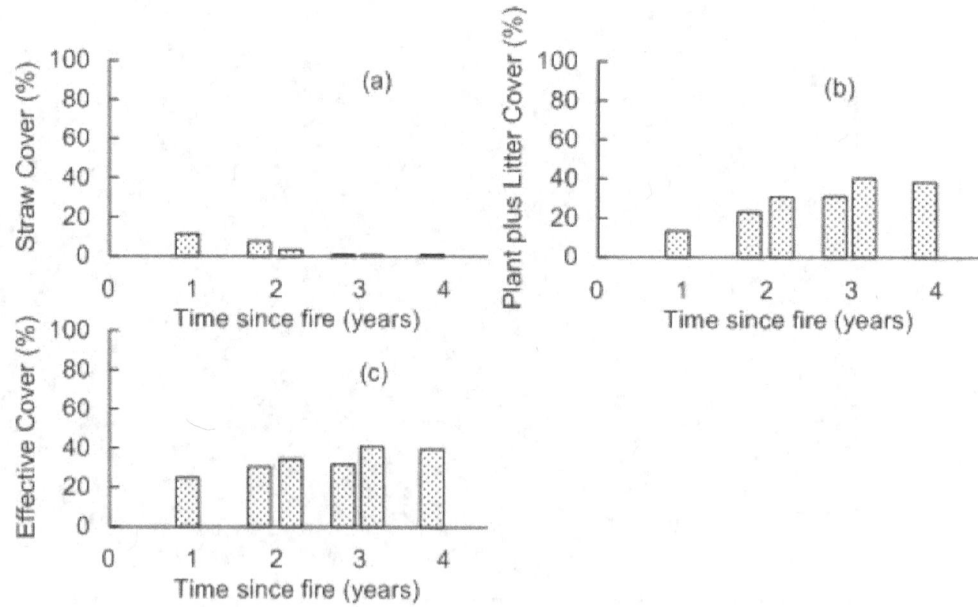

Figure 7—Upland ground cover vs. time on Tripod Complex Fires: (a) incidental straw cover, (b) average plant plus litter cover, and (c) effective ground cover (straw plus plant plus litter).

Soil loss from the cutslopes at the end of 3 years averaged 0.95 tons mi^{-1} (0.54 kg km^{-1}) of road length on the control compared to 0.46 tons mi^{-1} (0.26 kg km^{-1}) on the hydromulch. The mixed model did not detect a statistically significant difference in the 3-year average soil loss between the control and the roadside hydromulch (fig. 8). Additionally, the treatment by year interaction did not detect any statistically significant difference among the treatments within each of the 3 years. The 3-year mitigation due to roadside hydromulch was 52 percent.

Burroughs and King (1989) observed that hydromulch applied at less than 60 percent ground cover did not achieve any reduction in sediment production on unburned cut and fill slopes. All of the road-related Tripod hydromulch applications were less than 60 percent. Rough (2007) reported ground applied hydromulch on 0.25- to 1.26-ac (0.1- to 0.5-ha) upland swales at the Hayman Fire in Colorado resulted in mitigation values of 17 to 19 percent in years one and two following the fire. Tripod roadside hydromulch applied to cutslopes produced comparable mitigation values. Cutslopes are typically poorer growing sites than upland swales. The seed mix in the Tripod roadside hydromulch may have been beneficial on the harsh cutslope sites.

Road Responses to Major Storms

During the 3 years of the study, all 42 of the locations studied were able to meet the BAER objectives. However, several road sections within 10 miles (16 km) of the study sites failed.

Storms of July 18 and 19, 2007—On July 19, 2007 a thunderstorm caused high flows on Boulder Creek (fig. 9) to erode a section of FS road 3700 located 6 miles from our FS road 3700 locations and 2 miles from our FS road 5009200 locations. None of our study locations were impacted by this series of storms. The nearest rain gauge (RG16) was 1.4 miles (2.3 km) southwest of the eroded section and in the drainage of Boulder Creek. On the previous day, July 18, precipitation at RG16 was 0.76 inches (1.9 cm) with 1-hour, 30-minute, and 15-minute intensities of 0.29, 0.56 and 0.76 inches h^{-1} (0.74, 1.4, and 1.9 cm h^{-1}), respectively. Both the depth and the individual intensities

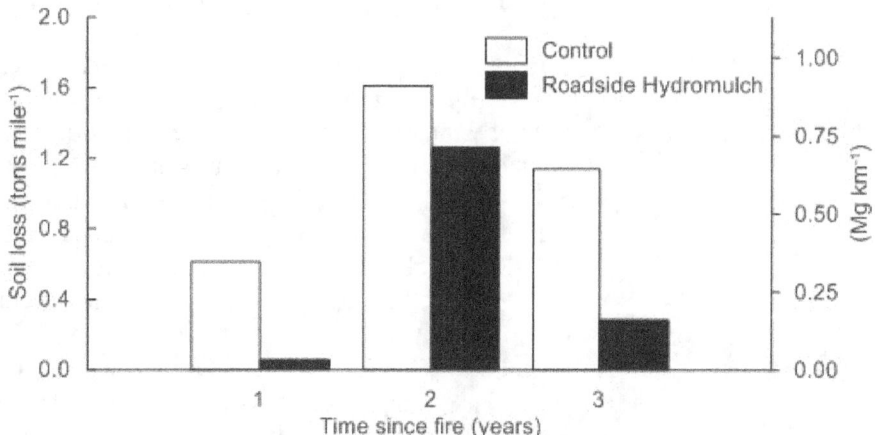

Figure 8—Soil loss from Tripod Complex Fires road cutslopes. Only in year one was there a statistically significant difference between control and hydromulch. Asterisks indicate statistically significant differences between control and roadside hydromulch.

USDA Forest Service Gen. Tech. Rep. RMRS-GTR-313. 2013

17

Figure 9—Boulder Creek below road washout on July 19, 2007, Tripod Complex Fires.

were the maximum for the year at the rain gauge. On the day of the high flow, July 19, RG16 measured 0.27 inches (0.69 cm) with 1-hour, 30-minute, and 15-minute intensities of 0.11, 0.22, and 0.28 inches h^{-1} (0.28, 0.56, and 0.71 cm h^{-1}), respectively. High soil water content from the previous day's precipitation combined with the precipitation of July 19 resulted in the high flows at Boulder Creek.

Winter of 2007-2008—The winter of 2007-2008 had 180 percent of normal snow packs in mid-April. In mid-May, rapidly warming temperatures caused the Methow River at Winthrop, Washington to peak at 300 percent of the mean daily flows. All of the study sites were able to accommodate the spring snowmelt period. Several sections on FS roads 3700 and 3900 failed and required repair. On FS road 3700, 0.6 miles uphill from our last location, a culvert failed resulting in a washout around the culvert (fig. 10). Our observation was that the angle between the culvert and the ditch was too sharp to allow the water to make the turn into the culvert, which caused water to erode around the culvert.

On FS road 3900 we observed extensive rilling on the running surface for 0.5 miles (0.8 km) on a steep section (~10 percent grade) descending from Freezeout Pass located between two of our measurement locations (fig. 11). Flow came off the cutslope, exceeded the capacity of the ditch, then flowed on the running surface causing multiple rills varying in width from 4 to 12 inches (10 to 30 cm) wide with depths up to 4 inches (10 cm) deep. The source of the cutslope flow was a ditch relief culvert on a spur road off FS road 3700.

Figure 10—Culvert failure on FS road 3700 following winter 2007-2008, Tripod Complex Fires.

Figure 11—Road failure on FS road 3900 below Freezeout Pass following winter 2007-2008, Tripod Complex Fires.

USDA Forest Service Gen. Tech. Rep. RMRS-GTR-313. 2013

19

At higher elevations within the Tripod Complex Fire perimeter, we observed impassable, heavily rilled road running surfaces (fig. 12). We surmised that during the rapid snowmelt the fill slope side of the running surface was snow-free while the cutslope and ditch side retained a snowpack. Snow melt ran at the edge of the snowpack and caused erosion in some places and sediment deposition in others (fig. 13). We observed similar occurrences of this phenomenon in several locations.

Winter 2008-2009—In the spring of 2009, FS road 3700800, Bromas Creek Road, was found to be essentially completely washed out due to snowmelt flowing on the running surface (fig. 14). Bromas Creek, a tributary to Boulder Creek, was between our FS road 5009200 and FS road 3700 locations. All of our measurement locations were able to accommodate the winter 2008-2009 snowmelt.

Implications for BAER road effectiveness design—The design philosophy was multiple repetitions of a treatment within a closely spaced area. The multiple repetitions (six) allowed a reasonable chance of detecting a statistically significant difference between treatments and subjected each of the repetitions to similar weather conditions. The road failures at locations near, but not at our chosen locations, indicated that this design philosophy was not sufficient to capture the widely spaced road failures that were observed. We changed our design philosophy in an attempt to capture the broader scale of road failures. We were able to implement this change at the Klamath Theater Complex Fires study.

Figure 12—Failures on FS road 3900 following winter 2007-2008, Tripod Complex Fires.

Figure 13—Sediment deposition along centerline of FS road 3700 following winter 2007-2008, Tripod Complex Fires. Location of sediment suggests that flow was at edge of snowpack on cutslope side of the road.

Figure 14—Washed out FS road 3700800 following winter 2007-2008, Tripod Complex Fires.

USDA Forest Service Gen. Tech. Rep. RMRS-GTR-313. 2013

21

Tripod Complex Summary

The 3-year period after the fire was dryer than normal. The maximum observed 1-hour rainfall intensity was less than the BAER team's 1-hour design storm. From our rain gauges we concluded that between a 2- and a 5-year return period, 1-hour storm was observed. While these conditions were favorable for the road treatments, they did not allow us a good opportunity to actually test whether or not the road treatments would perform effectively under the BAER team's design storm. This observation is an important consideration when evaluating the observed effectiveness discussed below.

We observed that a 0.6-inch h^{-1} (15-mm h^{-1}), 30-minute duration rainstorm was required to produce surface runoff from the high soil severity burn area above the road in the year after the fire. A similar rainstorm in year two did not produce runoff.

We observed no rutting in any of the aggregate nor in any of the native surface sections after 2400 to 4000 vehicle passes. Both aggregate surfacing and native surfacing achieved the goal of minimizing the concentration of surface runoff by eliminating wheel rut formation.

The drain dips were somewhat longer and deeper than the forest's specification. None of the drain dips failed. The drain dips with armor were also somewhat longer and deeper than the forest's specification. The armor rock was within the size specification and did not move during the study period.

A culvert upgrade on a stream base flow of 0.3 cfs (0.008 m^3 s^{-1}) was necessary to accommodate the post-fire flow. Three of the culvert upgrades did not occur, which leads us to observe that the original size culvert was sufficient to accommodate the observed post-fire flows. Two of the six culvert upgrades that we monitored did not show any evidence of flow. Thus, two of the six upgrades were not necessary. We suggest that many of the Tripod culvert upgrades were not justified by the observed post-fire flows.

The ditch treatments resulted in shallower and wider ditches that the forest's specification. The ditches cleaned to a depth of about 1 ft immediately after the fire were sufficient to pass the post-fire flows for the 3-year study period.

The placement of class 3 riprap rock around culvert inlets and outlets resulted in no failures. Three of our six sites did not receive the planned riprap rock placement. Of the three remaining sites with riprap rock, only one received any flow to test the riprap. We suggest that many of the Tripod riprap rock placements were not justified by the observed post-fire flows.

Roadside hydromulch placement on cutslopes was effective in reducing cumulative 3-year soil loss by 52 percent compared to bare conditions. There was no statistically significant difference in the soil loss from the roadside hydromulch compared to the control. The seed in the hydromulch did not result in statistically significant higher effective ground cover than sections without hydromulch. Plants on hydromulch sections were predominantly grasses while forbs dominated the no-treatment, originally bare sections.

The fact that there were several road failures that our closely spaced, multiple repetitions design philosophy were not able to capture lead us to change our subsequent design to a widely spaced, multiple repetitions one. This change was implemented at the Klamath Theater Complex study.

Introduction

The Cascade Complex Fires on the Payette National Forest and the Boise National Forest began 17 July 2007 and burned over 200,000 acres (81,000 ha) of land area containing designated critical habitat for three Endangered Species Act (ESA) aquatic species—Chinook salmon, steelhead, and bull trout—in central Idaho before it was contained after the first large snowfall. The vegetation types were Whitebark pine (*Pinus albicaulis*)/subalpine fir, Douglas-fir/snowberry (*Symphoricarpos albus*); and Ponderosa pine (*Pinus ponderosa*)/snowberry. Soil burn severities were 38 percent high, 39 percent moderate, and 23 percent low (USDA Forest Service 2007). Dominant soils were typic and lithic Cryocherepts and Cryothents and Cryumbrepts Xeropsamments derived from granodiorite and granites of the Idaho batholith. The transportation system that was affected consisted of 13 mi (21 km) of roads. The road emergency treatment objective was (1) to protect life and road infrastructure associated with erosion control and water management structures that were damaged or destroyed by the fire, (2) to provide the sole road access in the winter to the community of Yellow Pine, and (3) to control erosion and mass failures along the road thus protecting ESA listed fish species. The BAER team selected a design storm duration of 24 hours with a storm magnitude of 2.0 inches (50 mm). Road recommendations consisted of (1) replacing 142 burned plastic culverts with metal; (2) repairing or replacing 41 wooden culvert inlet retaining walls; (3) treating cut and fill slopes with wood fiber mulch, straw mulch, PAM-12 soil amendment; (4) hydroseeding 210 acres (85 ha) of cutslopes; (5) planting 1600 native shrub species on cut and fill slopes; (6) clearing imminent hazardous downfall and rocks from road inslope ditches and cutslopes; and (7) replacing 30 damaged road safety and warning signs for a total of $802,124.

We collaborated with the Payette National Forest in a study to (1) determine the effectiveness of road treatments on stabilizing road cuts and fills and drainage system functions, and (2) determine the effectiveness of three mitigation treatments (WoodStraw™, straw mulch with tackifier, and PAM-12) and a control (no treatment) on reducing hillslope erosion. The experimental design was a randomized block consisting of five treatments randomly applied at three road locations in a high soil burn severity for a total of 30 plots. The five treatments were the original recommendations of control, straw mulch, Woodstraw™, and a combination of straw mulch, tackifier, and Woodstraw™, which we shall refer to as SWT. We had an opportunity to test PAM-12 erosion control agent so it was added to the original BAER recommendations. Two of the three roads were non-system, native surface, 1950s vintage timber harvest roads known as the Twin Creek Road and the Poverty Overlook Road. The third road was the South Fork Salmon River Road (674), which is a paved single-lane road (fig. 15).

Plot installation began in September 2007. Data collection continued until the fall of 2011. The cutslope plots were installed with a silt fence sediment collector at the base of the slope without side borders (Robichaud and Brown 2002). Plots with upland above the cutslope that we thought would contribute runoff had a water diversion ditch or barrier installed. Because of aerial application of straw mulch to the burned area above the cutslopes, five of the plots were rendered unacceptable for the study so the final experimental design was not the intended full randomized block design (table 12). Table 13 shows selected plot characteristics.

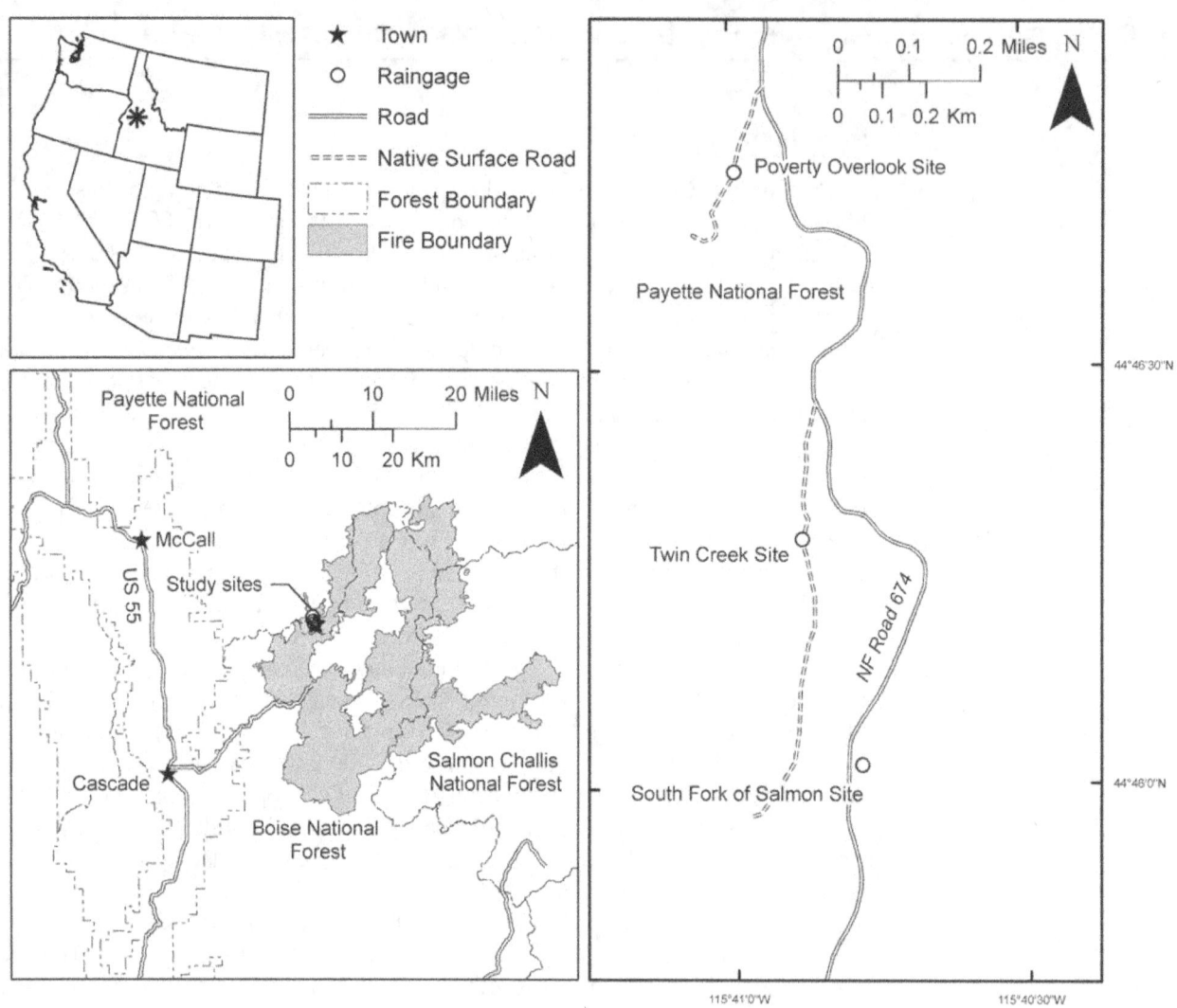

Figure 15—Map of Cascade Complex Fires showing study locations.

Table 12—Final experimental design on Cascade Complex BAER Road Effectiveness Study.

Road	Control	PAM-12	Straw	Woodstraw™	SWT	Road Total
Twin Creek	1	0	2	1	2	6
Poverty Overlook	2	2	2	3	0	9
South Fork Salmon	2	2	2	0	3	9
TOTAL	5	4	6	4	5	24

NOTE: A full factorial design would have had 2 of each of the treatments at each road for a road total of 10 and a total of 6 of each of the treatments for a grand total of 30.

Table 13—Cutslope plot characteristics on Cascade Complex BAER Road Effectiveness Study.

Road	Elevation	Slope	Height	Aspect
	(ft [m])	*(percent)*	*(ft [m])*	
Twin Creek	5115 [1600]	83	17 [5.3]	East
Poverty Overlook	5025 [1530]	93	21 [6.3]	East
South Fork Salmon	4900 [1490]	95	17 [5.3]	West

USDA Forest Service Gen. Tech. Rep. RMRS-GTR-313. 2013

Control plots were not treated with any erosion control material. PAM-12 was applied at a rate of 505 lbs ac^{-1} (570 kg ha^{-1}). Straw mulch was applied at a targeted rate of 550 lbs ac^{-1} (620 kg ha^{-1}) with an addition of 50 to 70 dry lbs ac^{-1} (60 to 80 dry kg ha^{-1}) of tackifier. Woodstraw™ was applied at a target rate 4000 lbs ac^{-1} (4500 kg ha^{-1}). The Woodstraw™ application rate was much higher because wood weighs about eight times that of straw mulch. The SWT target rate was not specified. Straw mulch and tackifier were applied first followed by the Woodstraw™. Percent ground cover was not specified for any of the treatments.

Ground cover on cutslopes was measured using digital photographs taken in September 2007, 2008, and 2010 using an overlay grid with 100 points per plot. The grid was scaled to represent 1 meter by 1 meter on the ground. Ground cover types were bare, mulch, rock, plant, or litter. Once PAM was applied to the ground it was not possible to see whether it was present; this resulted in treatment cover for PAM being recorded as zero thus introducing a bias into the treatment cover and effective ground cover for PAM.

Silt fences were cleaned of accumulated sediment after every major storm for the duration of the study. Wet sediment weight was measured in the field and later corrected for moisture content based on a sample that was oven dried overnight at 110 °C (ASTM 2000).

A mixed model investigated the effect of treatments (control, PAM, straw mulch, Woodstraw™, and SWT), the effect of time (years one through four), and the interactions among treatments and time (how treatments changed with time). The soil loss from each of the cutslope mitigation techniques compared to that of a control was analyzed using a general linear mixed model (Littell 2006). Treatments were fixed effects. Random effects were blocks, treatment by block interaction, treatment by block interaction within road, and year by treatment by block interaction. Least squares means were adjusted using the Tukey-Kramer Honest Significant Difference (HSD) to detect paired differences. A 95 percent confidence level was used for both the mixed model and the HSD adjustments. After a fourth root transformation, the mixed model assumed a Gaussian distribution for the soil loss.

A generalized linear mixed model with fixed and random effects, similar to the soil loss analysis, was used to investigate (1) how plant plus litter changed over time, (2) how mulch plus plant and litter changed over time, and (3) how mulch impacted plant regeneration. No transformation of plant, litter, or mulch was required. Analysis did not include PAM-12 due to the cover count bias.

Precipitation

Installation of one rain gauge for each road was completed in September 2007. All of the rain gauges were operational during the three summers of the study (table 14). The Long Valley SNOTEL site was 20 mi (32 km) west and at the same elevation as the study site. Summer precipitation was above average ranging from 88 to 182 percent of the 10-year average.

Table 14—Summer precipitation at Twin Creek, Poverty Overlook, South Fork Salmon River, and Long Valley SNOTEL. Values for the SNOTEL site are a 10-year average beginning in 2002.

Location	Year one summer 1 Apr to 31 Oct 2008		Year two summer 1 Apr to 31 Oct 2009		Year three summer 1 Apr to 31 Oct 2010	
	Precip	Days w/precip	Precip	Days w/precip	Precip	Days w/precip
	(in [mm])		(in [mm])		(in [mm])	
Twin Creek	9.0 [230]	59	14.1 [360]	69	18.9 [480]	92
Poverty Overlook	8.1 [200]	60	9.1 [230]	50	17.5 [450]	88
S. Fork Salmon	8.2 [210]	57	14.0 [46]	67	15.7 [400]	80
Long Valley SNOTEL	9.6 [240]	---	9.6 [240]	---	9.6 [240]	---

USDA Forest Service Gen. Tech. Rep. RMRS-GTR-313. 2013

25

The maximum 1-hour intensity was 0.55 inches h^{-1} (14 mm h^{-1}) on the South Fork Salmon road on 2 April 2010 (table 15). TP-40 estimates this as a 5-year return period event. The BAER team's design storms were 2-hour, 1.2 inch (2-hr, 30 mm) and a 6-hour, 1.8 inch (6-hr, 46 mm). No storms had duration-depths of this magnitude. The largest 2-hour storm was 0.94 inches (24 mm) on 2 April 2010 and the largest 6-hour storm was 1.53 inches (39 mm) on 19 October 2007. Based on TP40, the design storms represent 50-year return period events and the observed precipitations were about 25-year return period events.

Cutslope Mulch Treatments

Initial cutslope mulch treatments ranged from a high of 84 percent ground cover for the straw mulch to a low of 63 percent for the Woodstraw™ (fig. 16a). After 3 years, all of the treatments had declined in a linear manner to approximately 25 percent ground cover. Vegetation cover in years three and four may have covered the mulches resulting in them being undercounted. The mixed model indicated a statistically significant difference between Woodstraw™ and straw mulch and between Woodstraw™ and SWT in year one indicating that the Woodstraw™ was applied at a lower initial cover than the straw mulch or SWT. After year one, there were no statistically significant differences in treatment cover among straw mulch, Woodstraw™, and SWT.

Plant plus litter cover—Plant plus litter cover on all the treatments (fig. 16b) reached a maximum at the end of the study ranging from a high of 66 percent on the PAM to a low of 29 percent on the Woodstraw™. The mixed model indicated a statistically significant difference in plant plus litter cover between the control and Woodstraw™ indicating that plant regrowth was slower on the sections treated with Woodstraw™. Plant regrowth on all the other treatments was not distinguishable from that on the control sections.

Effective ground cover—The combination of mulch treatment cover and plant plus litter constitutes effective ground cover. One year after the fire, the control and PAM effective ground cover averaged 23 percent compared to 74 percent for straw mulch, Woodstraw™, and SWT (fig. 16c). Three years after the fire, the range of all the treatments was 53 percent on the control to 73 percent on both the straw mulch and SWT.

The mixed model indicated that the effective ground cover was statistically significant between control and all the other treatments (PAM was excluded from the analysis) and that the straw mulch and Woodstraw™ were statistically different. Thus, the treatments

Table 15—Maximum 1-hour, 30-minute, and 15-minute rainfall intensities. Values in **bold** denote maximum observed for a given road.

Road	Year	Max 1-hour		Max 30 min		Max 15-minute	
		(in h^{-1} [mm h^{-1}])	*Date*	*(in h^{-1} [mm h^{-1}])*	*Date*	*(in h^{-1} [mm h^{-1}])*	*Date*
Twin Creek	1	**0.49 [12]**	**8 Aug 2008**	**0.92 [23]**	**8 Aug**	**1.72 [44]**	**8 Aug**
	2	0.28 [7]	13 Jul 2009	0.54 [14]	13 Jun	0.80 [20]	13 Jun
	3	0.30 [8]	4 Jun 2010	0.50 [13]	9 Aug	1.00 [25]	9 Sep
Poverty Overlook	1	**0.39 [10]**	**8 Aug 2008**	**0.76 [19]**	**8 Aug**	**1.20 [30]**	**8 Aug**
	2	0.31 [8]	6 Jun 2009	0.60 [15]	13 Jun	1.04 [26]	13 Jun
	3	0.33 [8]	15 Jun 2010	0.34 [9]	15 Jun	0.56 [14]	15 Jun
South Fork Salmon	1	0.37 [9]	8 Aug 2008	0.52 [13]	8 Aug	0.60 [15]	20 Oct
	2	0.31 [8]	4 Jun 2009	0.62 [16]	4 Jun	0.76 [19]	5 Aug
	3	**0.55 [14]**	**2 Apr 2010**	**1.08 [27]**	**2 Apr**	**2.16 [55]**	**2 Apr**

USDA Forest Service Gen. Tech. Rep. RMRS-GTR-313. 2013

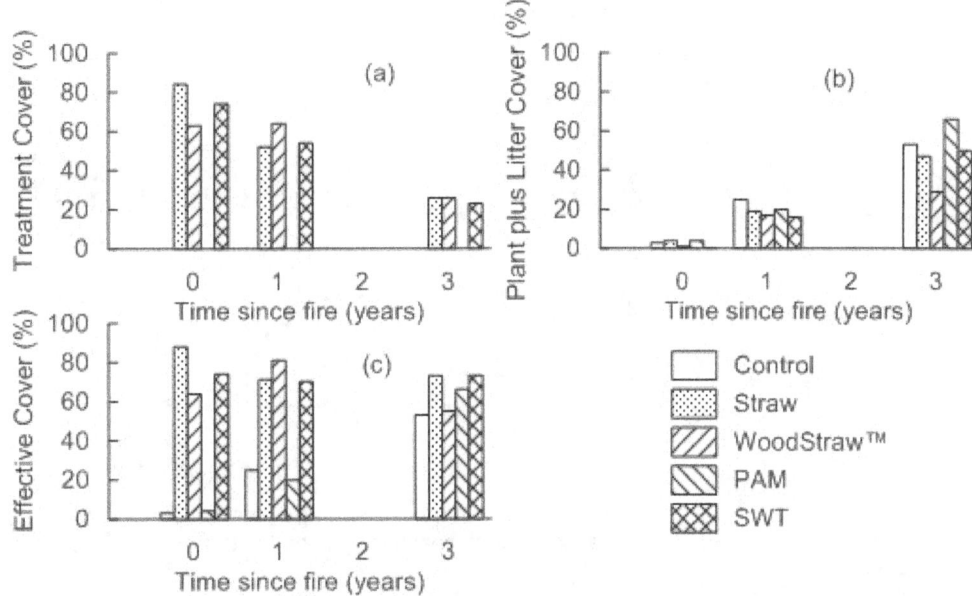

Figure 16—Cutslope cover at Cascade Complex Fires. There were no statistically significant annual pairwise comparisons among the treatments in (a) or (b). In (c) at year 0, all pairwise comparisons with the control except with PAM were statistically significant; all pairwise comparisons with PAM except with the control were statistically significant; and the pairwise comparison between straw and WoodStraw™ was statistically significant. In (c) at year one, the pairwise comparison between PAM and straw and the pairwise comparison between PAM and WoodStraw™ were statistically significant differences. In (c) at year three, there were no statistically significant pairwise differences.

did not provide the same degree of 3-year effective ground cover with straw mulch providing the highest level and Woodstraw™ providing the lowest. The treatment by year interaction indicated that each pair-wise comparison in both year zero and year one was statistically significant. In these initial years, each treatment provided statistically different amounts of effective ground cover from each other as well as from the control. The order of decreasing effective ground cover was straw mulch, SWT, Woodstraw™, and control. By year three, the Woodstraw™ was statistically different from both the straw mulch and the SWT while all other pair-wise combinations were not statistically different. After 2 years, natural re-vegetation had eliminated any effective ground cover advantage offered by the straw mulch or SWT. Sections treated with Woodstraw™ had statistically lower effective ground cover after 3 years, suggesting that, at the Cascade Complex Fire, re-vegetation on Woodstraw™ treated sections was less effective than on the other treatments.

Soil loss—Soil loss from the cutslopes at the end of 4 years was highest from the control at 840 tons mi^{-1} (470,000 kg km^{-1}) of road and lowest from the straw mulch at 210 tons mi^{-1} (120,000 kg km^{-1}) of road (fig. 17). Between 88 and 96 percent of the cumulative sediment occurred in the first year after the fire.

The mixed model indicated that soil loss from the control was significantly higher than the straw mulch. None of the treatments (straw mulch, SWT, PAM, or Woodstraw™) resulted in soil loss values that were significantly different from one another. Thus, for the 4 years following the fire our study could conclude that only the straw mulch statistically outperformed the control. The treatment by year interaction indicated no statistically significant differences.

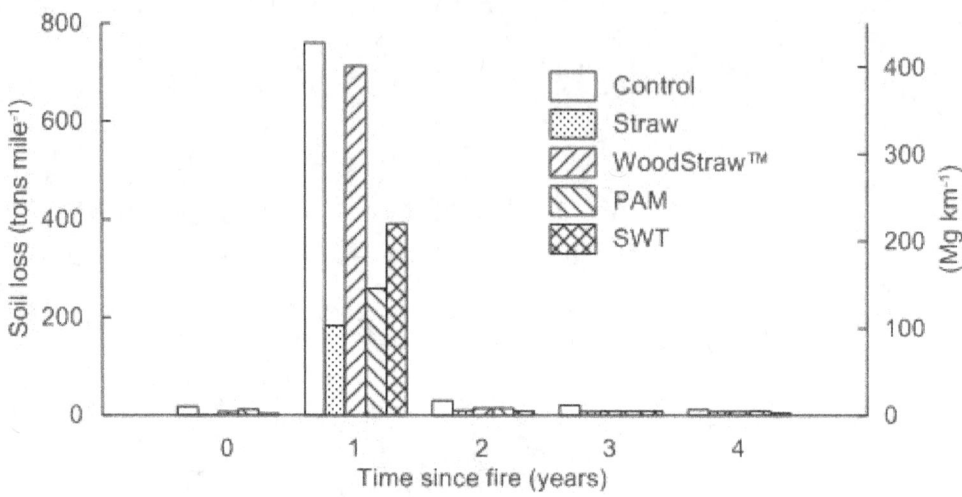

Figure 17—Soil loss from cutslopes, Cascade Complex Fires. There were no statistically significant annual pairwise comparisons among the treatments.

The choice of an incomplete factorial design of six plots on a total of three roads to distinguish the difference among five treatments combined with a coefficient of variation ranging from 90 to 250 percent between plots with the same treatment was not sufficient to distinguish treatment by year interaction for soil loss values. This inability to distinguish among treatments does not mean the treatments are identical, but that the variability between treatments is not different from the background or error variability. Such results are a common outcome for low power designs such as these. Additionally, to have been effective erosion control agents, the steep cutslopes may have required higher application rates of the mulch treatments than were applied.

Sediment mitigation—The only statistically significant pairwise comparison that included the control treatment was control vs. straw mulch; this limits the ability to determine meaningful sediment mitigation values for the other mulch treatments. The sediment mitigation of straw mulch compared to the control treatment was 76 percent, which is compatible with those reported by Burroughs and King (1989), Dean (2001), Wagenbrenner and others (2006), and Foltz (2012).

A window of vulnerability for high soil loss occurs when effective ground cover is low and rainfall intensity is high. For post-fire road treatments, this corresponds to the time required for vegetation to re-establish on the adjacent upland forest. One to 2 years are sufficient to re-establish 50 percent vegetation in quick recovering locations (Wohlgemuth and others 2010) while 3 to 4 years are required in less favorable locations, such as southern California following winter rains or portions of Colorado, Montana, and Idaho (Robichaud and others 2009). At the Cascade Complex Fires, effective ground cover was low on the control and PAM treatments in year one but essentially equal on all treatments at 50 percent by year three. The highest rainfall intensity occurred on two of the three road locations in year one, which resulted in the highest soil loss occurring in year one. It is interesting to note that the highest rainfall intensity (2 inches h[-1] [50 mm h[-1]], 15-minute duration) during the study occurred in year three. By that time the effective ground cover had reached 50 to 75 percent on all treatments, which resulted in a small soil loss suggesting that 50 percent ground cover was sufficient to mitigate soil loss.

Cascade Complex Summary

The 3-year precipitation after the fire was above average ranging from 88 to 182 percent of the long term. The BAER team chose two design storms of 2-hour, 1.2 inch (30 mm) and 6-hour, 1.8 inch (46 mm). No storms had duration-depths of this magnitude. The 2-hour and the 6-hour observed storms were about 25-year return period events. While the design storms were not observed, the post-fire precipitation did allow for a more rigorous test of the post-fire road treatments than at the Tripod Complex and the Klamath Theater Complex Fires.

The ground cover provided by the sediment control treatments of straw mulch, Woodstraw™, and SWT all declined from their initial values of 84 to 63 percent to nearly 25 percent by the end of 3 years. Plant re-growth was statistically slowest on the Woodstraw™ while the other sediment control treatments were not statistically different from the control. The straw mulch provided the highest effective ground cover and the control the lowest with each of the sediment control treatments statistically greater than the control.

Straw mulch resulted in statistically less soil loss than control. None of the sediment control treatments were statistically distinguishable from each other. The limitation of the experimental design reduced the ability to detect differences among the treatments.

USDA Forest Service Gen. Tech. Rep. RMRS-GTR-313. 2013

29

Introduction

The Klamath Theater Complex Fires on the Klamath National Forest in northern California consisted of the Siskiyou, Panther, Panther (Oct), Caribou, and Slinkard fires. These fires started between 20 June and 17 August 2008 and ultimately burned 93,000 acres (38,000 ha). The vegetation types were Douglas-fir, Ponderosa pine, canyon live oak (*Quercus chrysolepis*), tanoak (*Lithocarpus densiflorus*), black oak (*Quercus kelloggii*), madrone (*Arbutus menziesii*), deerbrush (*Ceanothus integerrimus*), and manzanita (*Arctostaphlos* spp.) Post fire burn severity mapping suggested 7 percent in the high, 22 percent moderate, and 29 percent low (USDA Forest Service 2008). Dominant soils were sandy loam derived from granitic parent material. The transportation system that was affected consisted of 147 miles (240 km) of roads. The road emergency treatment objective was to mitigate the increased threat to roads, culverts, and bridges because of higher runoff and the likelihood that these facilities would plug, overtop, or wash away. The BAER report (USDA Forest Service 2008) states "These roads were installed at very steep grades (>7 percent) and straightened using large fills across intermittent channels. Many of these intermittent stream crossings have small, 18-inch culverts installed at the bottom of each fill." The BAER team selected a design storm duration of 6 hours with a storm magnitude of 3.0 inches (76 mm). Road recommendations consisted of 12 treatments at a total cost of $382,000.

We collaborated with the Klamath National Forest in a study to (1) monitor how selected post-fire road treatments perform and determine if treatments met objectives by observing how treatments respond to rainfall and snowmelt precipitation events for 3 years following the fire, and (2) to validate the methodology initially developed at the Tripod Complex Fires in Washington State to assess the effectiveness of post-fire road treatments. The BAER team identified "large fills with small 18-inch culverts draining intermittent drainages" as one of the highest post-fire road risks (USDA Forest Service 2008). This study focused on detailed measurements of culverts and catch basin characteristics to perform a "before" and "after" assessment of these stream crossing characteristics in the event of a failure.

The duration of the study was 3 years beginning in the fall of 2008 with installation of the weather station and detailed measurement of culvert basins completed in late November 2008. We limited our study to areas that experienced moderate to high soil burn severity. There were no sites on either the Slinkard or Caribou Fires because they did not meet our selection criteria (fig. 18).

On the Panther Fire, we measured culverts and catch basins on FS roads 15N17Y (10.6 mi [17.1 km]). On the Panther (Oct) Fire, culverts and catch basins were measured on FS roads 15N06 (2.1 mi [3.4 km]) and 15N03 (2.8 mi [4.5 km]). These three roads ranged in elevation from 2,480 to 4,560 ft (760 to 1,390 m). The North Siskiyou Fire had 1.10 mi (1.8 km) of culverts and catch basins surveyed on FS road 15N19 with an elevation range from 4,240 to 4,420 ft (1,290 to 1,350 m). On the South Siskiyou Fire, we measured culverts and catch basins on FS roads 13N10 (0.2 mi [0.3 km]) and 15N21 (1.3 mi [2.1 km]) covering a range of elevation from 4,400 to 4,600 ft (1,340 to 1,400 m). We measured culvert diameter, slope, catch basin top width, height, and depth; and road width and fill slope, and drainage slope. Each of the roads had at least one rain gauge and at least one stream gauge with a weather station located near the upper end of the 15N03 road.

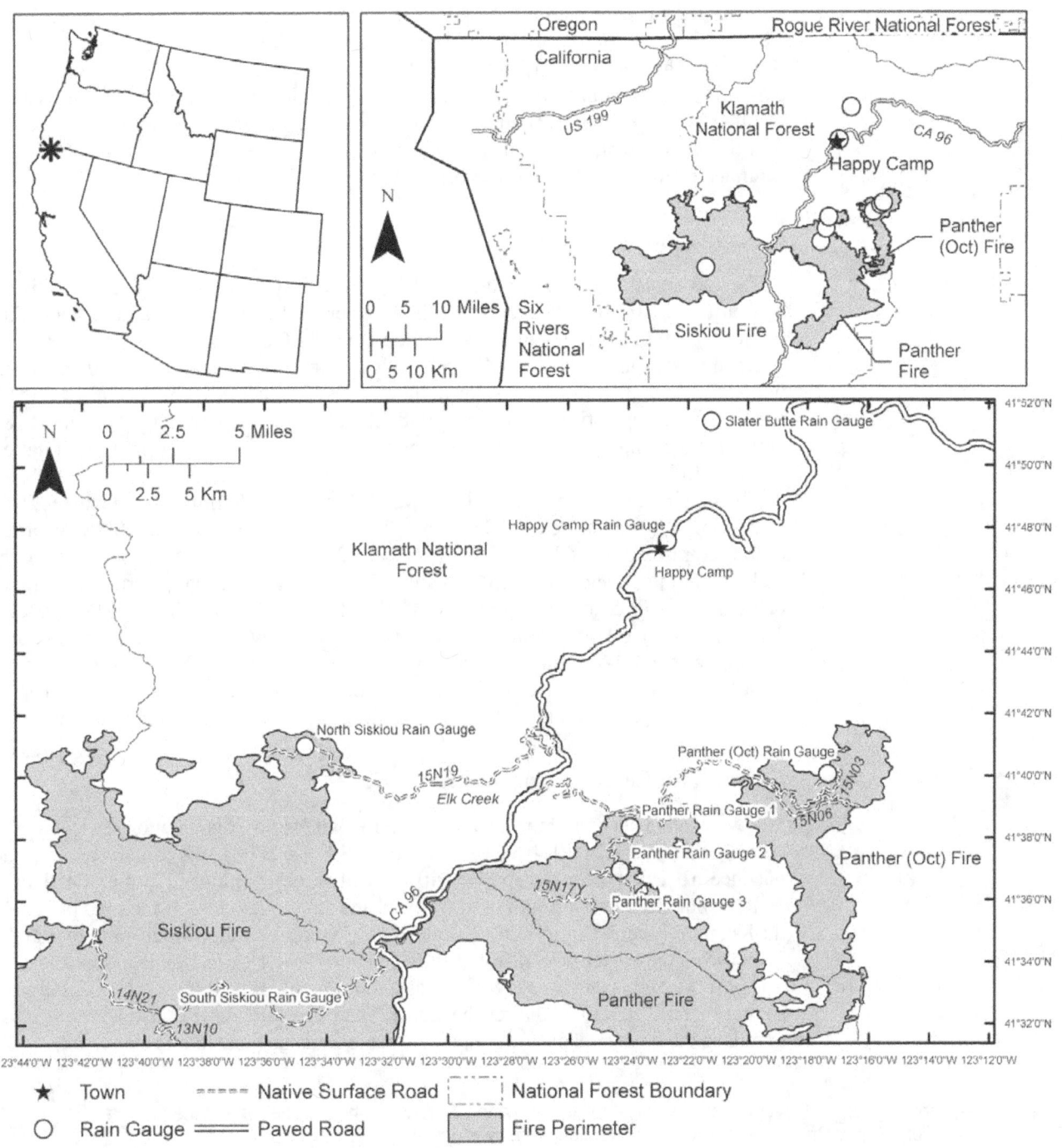

Figure 18—Map of the Klamath Complex Fires showing study locations.

USDA Forest Service Gen. Tech. Rep. RMRS-GTR-313. 2013

31

Soils in the North and South Siskiyou areas were predominately gravelly loams with a United Classification System GM class in a metamorphic, granitic, or serpentinite rock residuum. The Panther and Panther (Oct) soils were predominately sandy loams, SM classification, from a residuum of granite. Previous fires on the granite residuum soils resulted in steep ephemeral and intermittent channels producing debris flows during runoff events. Stream crossing road fills in these soils were often highly unstable when saturated resulting in debris flows originating on the road prism.

Precipitation

We had a total of six rain gauges in the study area with one on the North Siskiyou, one on the South Siskiyou, three on the Panther, and one on the Panther (Oct) Fire (table 16). All of the rain gauges were operational by the week of 16 November 2008. A weather station that recorded precipitation, humidity, temperature, soil moisture, wind speed and direction, and solar radiation was installed near the end of the 15N03 road and began operation 30 October 2008. Summer precipitation ranged from 56 to 81 percent of the long term average indicating another series of below normal precipitation in a post-fire setting.

The maximum 6-hour rainfall depth was 1.37 inches (35 mm) on 24 October 2010 in the South Siskiyou area. In October 2009 and again in October 2010 we recorded 6-hour storm depths of 1 to 1.1 inches (25 to 28 mm) in the North Siskiyou, South Siskiyou, Panther, and Panther (Oct) areas. These duration-depths were considerably below the BAER team's design storm of 3 inches (76 mm) in 6 hours. TP-40 rates a 3-inch (76 mm), 6-hour storm as a 5-year return period event and a 1.5-inch (38 mm), 6-hour storm as a 1-year return period event. As occurred at the Tripod Complex Fires, these storms were favorable for the road treatments, but did not allow a good test of their ability to perform under the expected high flow post-fire runoff conditions.

Culvert and Catch Basin Characteristics

Seventy-five percent of the culverts were 18 inch (46 cm) diameter or less (table 17). As discussed by the BAER team (USDA Forest Service 2008), this culvert size was one of concern because of the high probability of them becoming plugged by post-fire debris, which would lead to overtopping of the road and subsequent loss of the road prism. At the Klamath Theater Complex Fires, catch basins were excavated much more than at the Tripod Complex Fires with many of the Klamath Theater catch basins as deep as 3 m. The purpose of this larger excavation was to hold runoff and allow settling of sediment so that it could be removed after the storm. The large catch basins also were intended to reduce the downstream flows much the same as dams located on rivers.

Table 16—Summer precipitation at Slater Butte is 14 miles north and 200 ft (60 m) higher in elevation than the Panther (Oct) location. Happy Camp precipitation is 30-year long term average.

Location	Year one summer 1 Jun to 30 Nov 2009		Year two summer 1 Jun to 30 Nov 2010		Year three summer 1 Jun to 30 Nov 2011	
	Precip	Days w/ precip	Precip	Days w/ precip	Precip	Days w/ precip
	(in [mm])		(in [mm])		(in [mm])	
N. Siskiyou	16.7 [420]	49	0.9[a] [20]	15a	b	b
S. Siskiyou	1.0[a] [26]	9	11.6[a] [290]	11[a]	1.6[a] [40]	12[a]
Panther	11.0 [280]	44	12.2[a] [310]	30[a]	1.8[a] [46]	12[a]
Panther (Oct)	8.4 [210]	50	12.5 [318]	41	7.4 [188]	30
Slater Butte	8.9 [230]	41	11.2 [280]	31	7.7 [190]	27
Happy Camp	13.8 [350]	13.8 [350]	13.8 [350]			

[a] Rain gauge data intermittent during this time.
[b] Rain gauge data missing during this time.

Table 17—Culvert and catch basin volume summary.

Area	Culvert sizes			Catch basin volume[a]			Elevation range
	Nr	Nr ≤ 18 in dia	Max	Nr	Min	Max	
			(in [ᴍ])		(ᴍ³ [m³])		(ᴍ[m])
N. Siskiyou	10	1	60 [152]	9	2 [1.5]	200 [150]	4270 to 4470 [1300 to 1360]
S. Siskiyou	15	12	24 [61]	8	2 [1.5]	50 [36]	4370 to 4610 [1330 to 1400]
Panther	28	21	54 [137]	10	6 [4.6]	260 [200]	2840 to 3460 [870 to 1050]
Panther (Oct)	67	56	54 [137]	61	2 [1.5]	920 [700]	2310 to 4600 [700 to 1400]
TOTAL	120	90	60 [152]	88	2 [1.5]	920 [700]	2310 to 4610 [700 to 1400]

[a] Volume calculated from measured basin topography and a horizontal plane originating at road surface level.

Road Responses to Major Storms

During the 3 years of the study, all 120 of the culverts and basins we measured were sufficient to prevent overtopping and subsequent loss of the road prism. Quick attention by the district road maintenance crew to keeping the basins cleaned out after storms contributed to this success. In year one, there were at least three rainfall events that caused catch basins to fill with water and sediment. In year two, there were at least two rainfall events that caused catch basins to fill while in year three we were not aware of any events that caused a similar road problem. Rainfall events with depths greater than 2 inches (50 mm) are listed in table 18 with road related impacts discussed below.

Table 18—Precipitation events with two day totals greater than 2 inches (50 mm).

Location	Year	Dates	Total Precip	Caused road problem?
			(in [mm])	
N. Siskiyou	1	None in 2008	---	---
	2	4 May 2009	3.20 [81]	Unknown
	2	13 & 14 Oct 2009	5.29 [134]	Yes
	3	None in 2010	---	---
S. Siskiyou	1	28 & 29 Dec 2008	4.18 [106]	a
	2	None in 2009	---	---
	3	13 & 14 Oct 2010	5.43 [139]	No
Panther	1	28 & 29 Dec 2008	4.46 [113]	a
	2	15 & 16 Mar 2009	4.25 [108]	Yes
	2	4 May 2009	2.03 [52]	No
	2	13 & 14 Oct 2009	3.71 [94]	Yes
	3	None in 2010	---	---
Panther (Oct)	1	27 & 28 Dec 2008	3.30 [84]	a
	2	4 May 2009	2.72 [69]	b
	2	28 May 2009	2.40 [61]	Yes
	2	31 Dec 2009	2.00 [51]	a
	3	2 Apr 2010	3.15 [80]	No
	3	27 Apr 2010	3.93 [100]	No

[a] Road problems from these late season events would likely not have been found until after the spring snowmelt.
[b] Road problems from this event were likely not found until after the 28 May event.

USDA Forest Service Gen. Tech. Rep. RMRS-GTR-313. 2013

33

Events of late November 2008—Prior to our installation of rain gauges, we observed flow on roads from the running surface over the fill slope on roads in the North Siskiyou, South Siskiyou, and the Panther areas. We also observed that some of the catch basins had standing water 2 weeks after major rain events (see fig. 19 for an example). None of the catch basins we monitored were damaged from this standing water. While there were fill slope failures on roads within the burn perimeter, none of them were on roads that we measured.

Events of 14, 15, and 16 March 2009—These events totaled 3.29 inches (84 mm) with 0.16 inches (4 mm) falling on the 14th, 1.89 inches (48 mm) on the 15th, and 1.24 inches (31 mm) on the 16th in the Panther area. We found a cutslope failure that blocked access near the end of the 15N17Y road. There were no other road impacts from these storms.

Event of 28 May 2009—This event totaled 2.40 inches (61 mm) in the Panther (Oct) area. It had 1-hr, 30-minute, and 15-minute rainfall intensities of 1.27, 1.98, and 2.72 inches h^{-1} (32, 50, and 69 mm h^{-1}). Our stream gauge 2 on the 15N06 road was physically removed by a debris flow. We estimated that the catch basin caught at least 72 yd^3 (55 m^3) of sediment after the 24 inch (61 cm) culvert failed to pass all of the debris flow causing sediment to drop out in the catch basin. The culvert did allow sufficient water to pass and thus prevented overtopping of the road prism. The district maintenance crew was able to remove the sediment and reshape the catch basin to near the original dimensions.

Events of 13 and 14 October 2009—The North Siskiyou rain gauge recorded 3.03 inches (77 mm) on 13 October and 2.26 inches (57 mm) on 14 October 2009. These events filled the 150 to 200 yd^3 (115 to 150 m^3) catch basins requiring the district maintenance crews to excavate and reshape them. Two catch basins on the North Siskiyou road 15N19 were designed to allow water to flow downhill in the roadside ditch to the next lower catch basin and exit under the road at that location. Following these October events a cutslope failure blocked this planned diversion and routed flow over the road fill causing the loss of a section of fill. The eroded section had to be repaired with heavy machinery.

The same frontal storm also affected the Panther (Oct) area, but our rain gauge at the weather station was not working because a bear destroyed it during the winter of 2009-2010. Overland flow and channel scour from the burned upland areas flowed into Elk Creek and caused high turbidity levels. The Happy Camp municipal water supply plant had to close for 48 hours until the creek cleared up. None of the Panther (Oct) area roads were impacted by these events.

Events of 28 and 29 March 2010—These events totaled 2.94 inches (75 mm) with 1.33 inches (34 mm) falling on the 28th and 1.61 inches (41 mm) on the 29th in the North Siskiyou area. Both pairs of connected basins had standing water covering collected sediment a month later during one of our visits.

Events of Spring 2011—The Happy Camp Ranger Station recorded 4.9 inches (126 mm) of precipitation in February with 15 and 16 February each exceeding a daily precipitation of 1.7 inches (43 mm). In early March four road failures were found on the 15N06 road. All of the failures originated in the road fill, were 60 to 75 ft (18 to 23 m) in length, and 5 to 13 ft (1.5 to 4 m) wide. Two of the failures had springs in or above the cutslope, which increased the saturation in the fills likely leading to failure. The remaining two failures had road surface water delivered to the fill, increasing the fill saturation and likely leading to the failure.

Figure 19—Catch basin before and after storms of early November 2008, Klamath Theater Complex Fires.

USDA Forest Service Gen. Tech. Rep. RMRS-GTR-313. 2013

35

Events of March 2012—The period from 15 to 31 March had a total of 12.39 inches (315 mm) with 15, 27, and 29 March each exceeding a daily precipitation of 2 inches (50 mm). This series of storms caused cut and fill slope failures in the Panther (Oct) area on the 15N06 and 15N03 roads. Several of the fill slope failures resulted in blocking vehicle passage. In addition to the fill slope failures, cracks in the running surface parallel to the fill indicated potential future full slope problems (fig. 20).

All these taken together indicate that the BAER treatments were sufficient to prevent the major concern of culverts plugging, flow overtopping the road prism, and erosion of the road prism. The BAER treatment where one basin was connected to the next lower one on the road failed to perform on one occasion when the connecting ditch was blocked by a cutslope failure. Regular post-storm maintenance to clean catch basins worked well.

Inspection of the events that resulted in sufficient overland flow to cause noticeable road maintenance problems suggests that storms of 2.5 inches (64 mm) per day were able to exceed the infiltration capacity of the burned upland soil and cause sufficient runoff to impact the road system. Every instance of a rainfall event greater than 2.5 inches (64 mm) in a day is discussed above.

The BAER team discussion (USDA Forest Service 2008) of possible road failure modes focused on culvert and catch basin problems caused by debris flows originating in swales above the road. However, many of the road related problems discussed above were a result of cutslope or fill slope failures rather than the expected culvert plugging or catch basin problems. The loss of evapotranspiration following the fires apparently resulted in an increase in the height of the water table above the roads. This higher water table caused new springs or seeps to develop in or above the cutslopes that lead to unstable road fill slopes and subsequent failures. At the Klamath Theater Complex Fires road locations, this mechanism appears to have been the predominate cause of post-fire road related failures.

Klamath Theater Complex Summary

The 3-year summer precipitation was below average. The maximum observed 6-hour storm was 1.1 inches (28 mm), which was below the BAER team's chosen design storm of 1.5 inches (38 mm). The observed 6-hour, 1.1 inch (28 mm) storm was approximately a 1-year return period event. As occurred at the Tripod Complex study site, these low intensity storms were favorable for the road treatments, but did not allow a good test of their ability to perform under the expected high flow post-fire conditions.

During the 3 years of the study, all 120 of the culverts and basins we monitored were of sufficient size to prevent overtopping of the roadway. Quick response by the district road maintenance crew helped keep the road infrastructure protected.

Our observations suggest that spring snowmelt combined with storms in excess of 2 inches (25 mm) in a day were able to raise the water table upslope from the roads, allow water to flow out of the cutslopes, and increase water saturation in the fill slopes leading to fill failures. This type of mass failure rather than the expected upslope mass failure removing road fills was the predominant post-fire road failure mechanism.

36

USDA Forest Service Gen. Tech. Rep. RMRS-GTR-313. 2013

Figure 20—Fill slope failures following March 2012 precipitation events, Klamath Theater Complex Fires.

USDA Forest Service Gen. Tech. Rep. RMRS-GTR-313. 2013

37

Two of the three locations had below average precipitation. All three had precipitation that did not meet the BAER team's design storm. All of the treatments we monitored at the three sites met the BAER team objectives. However, none of them were tested to the extent anticipated.

At the Tripod Complex and the Klamath Theater Complex, the fires occurred during an extended period of drought. Because the fires themselves do not affect the long term climate, one would expect the drought conditions to continue after the fire, which they did at two of the three locations. This suggests to us that BAER team design storm selection and subsequent treatment recommendations acknowledge this observation.

All three of our locations had large soil loss in year one with quick recovery of ground cover to 40 to 50 percent at the end of year one. Soil loss from roadside hydromulch was not statistically significant from control at the Tripod Complex sites. At the Cascade Complex sites, soil loss was statistically significant between the straw mulch and the control. There was no pairwise differences among the straw mulch, PAM, and Wood-Straw™ sediment control treatments. These findings suggest that amount of cover is more important than the type of cover for fast recovering locations. At slower recovering locations, the longer lasting treatments might have an advantage.

We began this study to determine the effectiveness of post-fire road treatments and to improve our methodology to make that assessment. Our initial methodology, which we used at the Tripod Complex, was to randomly select treatments in a small geographic area and make detailed topographic surveys of the treatments. If a failure of one the selected treatments occurred, we would make another detailed topographic survey and compare the before and after conditions with the intent of gleaning important details that contributed to the road treatment failure. When there were several road treatments failures near our sites, but none of our sites failed, we realized that this methodology was unsatisfactory.

The principal lesson from the Cascade Complex Fires was reinforcing the value of a well-thought-out experimental design. Our incomplete factorial design to determine the effectiveness of five treatments did not have sufficient statistical power to achieve the goal. As a result, we increased the number of repetitions at the Klamath Theater Complex Fires study.

The Klamath Theater study allowed us to try a different approach from highly detailed topographic measurements on a few randomly chosen sites to lower detail measurements on an entire road network. By monitoring a more widely spaced area, we hoped to observe road treatment failures and compare our before and after measurements to glean import details that contributed to the failures. Although we think this methodology was an improvement, low precipitation and no road treatment failures that we had measured again did not allow us to make an assessment of factors contributing to road treatment failures.

Three studies and 5 years after we began the effort, we think the best approach to assessing the effectiveness of post-fire BAER road treatments is a slight modification and a wider application of the Klamath Theater approach. A little knowledge of many sites would be better than a lot of knowledge of a few sites. Monitoring long road networks would increase the likelihood of capturing a failure.

References

American Society for Testing and Materials (ASTM). 2000. D 2216-98: Test method for laboratory determination of water (moisture) content of soil and rock by mass. West Conshohocken, PA: American Society for Testing and Materials.

Burroughs, E.R., Jr. and J.G. King. 1989. Reduction of soil erosion on forest roads. Gen. Tech. Rep. INT-264. Ogden, UT: U.S. Department of Agriculture, Forest Service, Intermountain Research Station. 21 p.

Calkin, D.E., K.D. Hyde, P.R. Robichaud, J. Jones, L.E. Ashmun, and D. Loeffler. 2007. Assessing post-fire values-at-risk with a new calculation tool. Gen. Tech. Rep. GTR-205. Fort Collins, CO: U.S. Department of Agriculture, Forest Service, Rocky Mountain Research Station. 32 p.

Dean, A.E. 2001. Evaluating effectiveness of watershed conservation treatments applied after the Cerro Grande Fire, Los Alamos, New Mexico. Tucson, AZ: University of Arizona. 116 p. Thesis.

DeBano, L.F., D.G Neary, and P.F. Ffolliot. 1998. Fire's effects on ecosystems. New York, NY: John Wiley & Sons. 333 p.

Foltz, R.B. 2012. A comparison of three erosion control mulches on decommissioned forest road corridors in the northern Rocky Mountains, USA. Journal of Soil and Water Conservation. 67(6): 536-544.

Foltz, R.B., P.R. Robichaud, and H. Rhee. 2009. A synthesis of post-fire road treatments for BAER teams: methods, treatment effectiveness, and decision making tools for rehabilitation. Gen. Tech. Rep. RMRS-GTR-228 Fort Collins, CO: U.S. Department of Agriculture, Forest Service, Rocky Mountain Research Station. 152 p.

Hershfield, David M. 1961. Rainfall frequency atlas of the United States for durations from 30 minutes to 24 hours and return periods from 1 to 100 years. Technical Paper 40. Washington, DC: U.S. Department of Commerce. 65 p.

Littell, R.C., G.A. Milliken, W.W. Stroup, R.D. Wolfinger, and O. Schabenberger. 2006. SAS for Mixed Models. Second Edition. Cary, NC: SAS Institute.

Miller, J.D., H.D. Safford, M. Crimmins, and A.E. Thode. 2009. Quantitative evidence for increasing forest fire severity in the Sierra Nevada and southern Cascade Mountains, California and Nevada, USA. Ecosystems. 12: 16-32. doi:10.1007/S10021-008-9201-9.

Napper, C. 2006. Burned Area Emergency Response Treatments Catalog. Tech. Rep. 0625 1801-SDTDC. Washington DC: U.S. Department of Agriculture, Forest Service, National Technology & Development Program, Watershed, Soil, Air Management. 253 p.

Robichaud, P.R. 2005. Measurement of post-fire hillslope erosion to evaluate and model rehabilitation treatment effectiveness and recovery. International Journal of Wildland Fire. 14(4): 475-485.

Robichaud, P.R., J.L. Beyers, and D.G. Neary. 2000. Evaluating the effectiveness of postfire rehabilitation treatments. Gen. Tech. Rep. RMRS-GTR-63. Fort Collins, CO: U.S. Department of Agriculture, Forest Service, Rocky Mountain Research Station. 85 p.

Robichaud, P.R. and R.E. Brown. 2002. Silt fences: an economical technique for measuring hillslope soil erosion. Gen. Tech. Rep. RMRS-GTR-94. Fort Collins, CO: U.S. Department of Agriculture, Forest Service, Rocky Mountain Research Station. 24 p.

Robichaud, P.R., J.W. Wagenbrenner, R.E. Brown, and K.M. Spigel. 2009. Three years of hillslope sediment yields following the Valley Complex fires, western Montana. Res. Pap. RMRS-RP-77. Fort Collins, CO: U.S. Department of Agriculture, Forest Service, Rocky Mountain Research Station. 8 p.

Robichaud, P.R., J.W. Wagenbrenner, and R.E. Brown. 2010. Rill erosion in natural and disturbed forests: 1. Measurements. Water Resources Research. 46: doi:10.1029/2009WR008314. 14 p.

Rough, D. 2007. Effectiveness of rehabilitation treatments in reducing post-fire erosion after the Hayman and Schoonover Fires, Colorado Front Range. Fort Collins, CO: Colorado State University. 186 p. Thesis.

Ruiz, L. 2005. Guidelines for road maintenance levels. Tech. Rep. 0577 1205-SDTDC. Washington DC: U.S. Department of Agriculture, Forest Service, National Technology & Development Program, Watershed, Soil, Air Management. 60 p

Shakesby, R.A., S.H. Doerr. 2006. Wildfire as a hydrological and geomorphological agent. Earth Science Reviews. 74: 269-307.

U.S. Department of Agriculture [USDA], Forest Service. 2006. Burned Area Emergency Response 2500-8 Report for the Tripod Fire. [Internal Report as per FSM 2523]. Available from: Okanogan-Wenatchee National Forest, Wenatchee, WA.

USDA Forest Service Gen. Tech. Rep. RMRS-GTR-313. 2013

39

U.S. Department of Agriculture [USDA], Forest Service. 2007. Burned Area Emergency Response 2500-8 Report for the Cascade Complex Fire. [Internal Report as per FSM 2523]. Available from: Payette National Forest, McCall, ID.

U.S. Department of Agriculture [USDA], Forest Service. 2008. Burned Area Emergency Response 2500-8 Report for the Klamath Theater Fires. [Internal Report as per FSM 2523]. Available from: Klamath National Forest, Yreka, CA.

Wagenbrenner, J.W., L.H. MacDonald, and D. Rough. 2006. Effectiveness of three post-fire rehabilitation treatments in the Colorado Front Range. Hydrological Processes. 20: 2989-3006.

Wohlgemuth, P.M., J.L. Beyers, and P.R. Robichaud. 2010. The effectiveness of aerial hydromulch as a post-fire erosion control treatment in southern California,. In: Proceedings of the Joint Federal Interagency Conference, 9th Federal Interagency Sedimentation Conference and 4th Federal Interagency Hydrologic Modeling Conference; June 27-July 1, 2010; Las Vegas, NV. 12 p.

Rocky Mountain Research Station

The Rocky Mountain Research Station develops scientific information and technology to improve management, protection, and use of the forests and rangelands. Research is designed to meet the needs of the National Forest managers, Federal and State agencies, public and private organizations, academic institutions, industry, and individuals. Studies accelerate solutions to problems involving ecosystems, range, forests, water, recreation, fire, resource inventory, land reclamation, community sustainability, forest engineering technology, multiple use economics, wildlife and fish habitat, and forest insects and diseases. Studies are conducted cooperatively, and applications may be found worldwide. For more information, please visit the RMRS web site at: www.fs.fed.us/rmrs.

Station Headquarters
Rocky Mountain Research Station
240 W Prospect Road
Fort Collins, CO 80526
(970) 498-1100

Research Locations

Flagstaff, Arizona	Reno, Nevada
Fort Collins, Colorado	Albuquerque, New Mexico
Boise, Idaho	Rapid City, South Dakota
Moscow, Idaho	Logan, Utah
Bozeman, Montana	Ogden, Utah
Missoula, Montana	Provo, Utah

Federal Recycling Program Printed on Recycled Paper

To learn more about RMRS publications or search our online titles:

www.fs.fed.us/rm/publications

www.treesearch.fs.fed.us